Brenda L. Underhill, MS, CAC
Dana G. Finnegan, PhD, CAC
Editors

Chemical Dependency: Women at Risk

*Pre-publication
REVIEWS,
COMMENTARIES,
EVALUATIONS . . .*

"This exciting collection of articles on chemical dependency and women *provides a comprehensive review of current and critical issues for women in recovery* . . . . most exciting is the presentation of the relational model as a theoretical framework for treating chemically dependent women combined with the richness of recommendations, strategies and approaches provided by very experienced and highly respected practitioners, researchers, trainers and policy-makers in the field . . . . *truly a beneficial and important volume for anyone concerned about positively impacting women in recovery.*"

Juana Mora, PhD
Professor, California State University

More pre-publication
REVIEWS, COMMENTARIES, EVALUATIONS . . .

"*Chemical Dependency: Women at Risk* offers an important collection of articles which speak to the wealth of knowledge we have about women with alcohol and other drug problems. The majority of writers in this important collection . . . . have over 20 years experience in the field of women and chemical dependency. The contributors *represent some of the best thinkers and actors in the national effort to provide women with alcohol and other drug problems the very real promise of recovery.* . . .

Just recently, the national news reported that the rate of women with alcohol and drug problems is beginning to closely parallel that of men. The news story also acknowledged that current prevention, intervention and treatment practices reflect very little awareness of the issues faced by women who use alcohol and other drugs, and the best strategies to respond to those issues. Those news reports were inaccurate. We know a great deal about how to treat women with chemical dependency and the people with that knowledge are the women who have been working with those women for a number of years.

[This] book will hopefully bring more visibility to the important insights contained in this book and will contribute to these views and practices being embraced by more and more treatment programs. The thoughtful and jargon-free analysis of Norma Finkelstein, informed by many years of clinical practice, will hopefully raise the visibility and practice of relational theory which acknowledges connections to family, friends and communities as a source of strength and empowerment for women. The modest and sometimes dated research data utilized throughout this book to support theses about women and chemical dependency also *conveys the urgent need for aggressive research on alcohol and other drug use among women of all ages, ethnic and racial orientations and sexual orientation. Chemical Dependency: Women at Risk makes a valuable contribution to the literature on women and addiction and, hopefully, will serve as a catalyst for even more of this vital and lifesaving work.*"

Christine Lubinski
Deputy Executive Director
AIDS Action, Washington, DC
formerly: Director for Public Policy
National Council on Alcoholism
and Drug Disorders

Chemical Dependency: Women at Risk

Chemical Dependency: Women at Risk

Brenda L. Underhill, MS, CAC
Dana G. Finnegan, PhD, CAC
Editors

The Haworth Press, Inc.
New York • London

Chemical Dependency: Women at Risk has also been published as *Journal of Chemical Dependency Treatment*, Volume 6, Numbers 1/2 1996.

The development, preparation, and publication of this work has been undertaken with great care. However, the publisher, employees, editors, and agents of The Haworth Press and all imprints of The Haworth Press, Inc., including The Haworth Medical Press and Pharmaceutical Products Press, are not responsible for any errors contained herein or for consequences that may ensue from use of materials or information contained in this work. Opinions expressed by the author(s) are not necessarily those of The Haworth Press, Inc.

The Haworth Press, Inc., 10 Alice Street, Binghamton, NY 13904-1580 USA

Library of Congress Cataloging-in-Publication Data

Chemical dependency: women at risk/Brenda L. Underhill, Dana G. Finnegan, editors.
     p. cm.
     "Has also been published as Journal of chemical dependency treatment, volume 6, numbers 1/2, 1996"–T.p. verso.
     Includes bibliographical references and index.
     ISBN 0-7890-0001-6 (alk. paper). -- ISBN 1-56023-088-6 (pbk. : alk. paper)
     1. Women–Drug use–United States. 2. Drug abuse–United States. 3. Substance abuse–Patients–Counseling of. I. Underhill, Brenda L. II. Finnegan, Dana G., 1932-   .
HV5824.W6C476 1996
362.29'12'082–dc20   96-33337
                                                                    CIP

This volume is dedicated to the memory of Carmella Woll who led, inspired and mentored so many of us. Her warmth, sense of hope, and courage were an inspiration.

Thank you, dear friend and colleague.

Brenda

INDEXING & ABSTRACTING

Contributions to this publication are selectively indexed or abstracted in print, electronic, online, or CD-ROM version(s) of the reference tools and information services listed below. This list is current as of the copyright date of this publication. See the end of this section for additional notes.

- *Academic Abstracts/CD-ROM,* EBSCO Publishing, P.O. Box 2250, Peabody, MA 01960-7250

- *ALCONLINE Database,* Swedish Council for Information on Alcohol and Other Drugs, Box 27302, S-102 54 Stockholm, Sweden

- *Brown University Digest of Addiction Theory and Application, The (DATA Newsletter),* Project Cork Institute, Dartmouth Medical School, 14 S. Main Street, Suite 2F, Hanover, NH 03755-2015

- *Cambridge Scientific Abstracts,* Environmental Routenet (accessed via INTERNET), 7200 Wisconsin Avenue #601, Bethesda, MD 20814

- *CNPIEC Reference Guide: Chinese National Directory of Foreign Periodicals,* P.O. Box 88, Beijing, Peoples Republic of China

- *Criminal Justice Abstracts,* Willow Tree Press, 15 Washington Street, 4th Floor, Newark, NJ 07102

- *Family Studies Database (online and CD-ROM),* Peters Technology Transfer, 306 East Baltimore Pike, 2nd Floor, Media, PA 19063

- *Health Source: Indexing & Abstracting of 160 selected health related journals, updated monthly,* EBSCO Publishing, 83 Pine Street, Peabody, MA 01960

- *Health Source Plus: expanded version of "Health Source" to be released shortly,* EBSCO Publishing, 83 Pine Street, Peabody, MA 01960

(continued)

- *Index to Periodical Articles Related to Law*, University of Texas, 727 East 26th Street, Austin, TX 78705

- *INTERNET ACCESS (& additional networks) Bulletin Board for Libraries ("BUBL"), coverage of information resources on INTERNET, JANET, and other networks.*
  - JANET X.29: UK.AC.BATH.BUBL or 00006012101300
  - TELNET: BUBL.BATH.AC.UK or 138.38.32.45 login 'bubl'
  - Gopher: BUBL.BATH.AC.UK (138.32.32.45). Port 7070
  - World Wide Web: http: / / www.bubl.bath.ac.uk./BUBL/ home.html
  - NISSWAIS: telnetniss.ac. uk (for the NISS gateway)
  The Andersonian Library, Curran Building, 101 St. James Road, Glasgow G4 ONS, Scotland

- *Medication Use STudies (MUST) DATABASE,* The University of Mississippi, School of Pharmacy, University, MS 38677

- *Mental Health Abstracts (online through DIALOG),* IFI/Plenum Data Company, 3202 Kirkwood Highway, Wilmington, DE 19808

- *NIAAA Alcohol and Alcohol Problems Science Database (ETOH),* National Institute on Alcohol Abuse and Alcoholism, 1400 Eye Street NW, Suite 600, Washington, DC 20005

- *Referativnyi Zhurnal (Abstracts Journal of the Institute of Scientific Information of the Republic of Russia),* The Institute of Scientific Information, Baltijskaja ul., 14, Moscow A-219, Republic of Russia

- *Social Work Abstracts,* National Association of Social Workers, 750 First Street NW, 8th Floor, Washington, DC 20002

- *Special Educational Needs Abstracts,* Carfax Information Systems, P.O. Box 25, Abingdon, Oxfordshire OX14 3UE, United Kingdom

- *Violence and Abuse Abstracts: A Review of Current Literature on Interpersonal Violence (VAA),* Sage Publications, Inc., 2455 Teller Road, Newbury Park, CA 91320

(continued)

SPECIAL BIBLIOGRAPHIC NOTES

related to special journal issues (separates)
and indexing/abstracting

❏ indexing/abstracting services in this list will also cover material in any "separate" that is co-published simultaneously with Haworth's special thematic journal issue or DocuSerial. Indexing/abstracting usually covers material at the article/chapter level.

❏ monographic co-editions are intended for either non-subscribers or libraries which intend to purchase a second copy for their circulating collections.

❏ monographic co-editions are reported to all jobbers/wholesalers/approval plans. The source journal is listed as the "series" to assist the prevention of duplicate purchasing in the same manner utilized for books-in-series.

❏ to facilitate user/access services all indexing/abstracting services are encouraged to utilize the co-indexing entry note indicated at the bottom of the first page of each article/chapter/contribution.

❏ this is intended to assist a library user of any reference tool (whether print, electronic, online, or CD-ROM) to locate the monographic version if the library has purchased this version but not a subscription to the source journal.

❏ individual articles/chapters in any Haworth publication are also available through the Haworth Document Delivery Services (HDDS).

Chemical Dependency: Women at Risk

CONTENTS

ABOUT THE EDITORS

Brenda L. Underhill, MS, CAC, is currently Senior Associate at Policy Research Incorporated in Bethesda, Maryland, where she provides technical assistance to federally funded alcohol and drug treatment programs for women and children. Her immediate past employment was at the Alcoholism Center for Women in Los Angeles. There she served as Clinical Director for one year and as Executive Director for 13 years. Ms. Underhill has been a service provider and activist on behalf of women with alcohol and other drug problems for over 20 years. During this time she has represented the interests of all women and has been diligent in her advocacy on behalf of lesbians and other underserved and unserved women. Ms. Underhill was core faculty for the Chemical Dependency Studies Program of the California Family Studies Center in North Hollywood for nine years (1984-1993). Her numerous activities have included serving as Chair of the Los Angeles Women's Alcohol Services Task Force, and service on the California Women's Initiative Committee and the California Women's Leadership Development Coalition. She has been a member of the Board of Directors of the California Women's Commision on Alcohol and Drug Dependencies, the California Association of Alcohol and Drug Program Executives, the Women's Action Alliance's National Advisory Board, Women's Alcohol Problems Prevention Project, and the National Association of Lesbian and Gay Alcoholism Professionals. In 1994 she received the National Association of State Alcohol and Drug Abuse Directors Career Achievement Award.

Ms. Underhill is a frequent and sought-after speaker and facilitator. She has testified on local and federal levels and published numerous articles on women's recovery from alcohol and drug problems. Her most recent publication, *Creating Visibility: Providing Lesbian Sensitive and Lesbian Specific Alcoholism Recovery Services,* is a handbook for traditional alcoholism and other drug addiction service providers on how to make their services lesbian-sensitive and lesbian-specific.

Dana G. Finnegan, PhD, CAC, is Co-Director of Discovery Counseling Center in Millburn, New Jersey, a center specializing in counseling services for individuals affected by alcoholism and sexual identity problems. She is a faculty member of the Rutgers University Center of Alcohol Studies Continuing Education Seminars, and Rutgers University Summer School of Alcohol Studies, where she has presented courses on the dynamics of supervision in alcoholism treatment agencies, practical group techniques and approaches for counseling alcoholics, teaching clients how to change and sexual identity issues in recovery.

Dr. Finnegan, currently a board member of the National Association of Lesbian and Gay Addiction Professionals (NALGAP), was Co-Founder and Co-National Coordinator of that organization.

She has written, with Emily McNally, *Dual Identities: Counseling Chemically Dependent Gay Men and Lesbians* (Hazelden, 1987), and with T. McGinnis, *Open Family and Marriage: A Guide to Personal Growth* (C. V. Mosby, 1976), as well as papers and articles on helping homosexual alcoholics. She has presented workshops and training seminars on counselors as change agents, group and individual counseling techniques, and counseling gay/lesbian alcoholics to regional and national conferences and organizations. She is an editorial board member of *Alcoholism Treatment Quarterly,* and is Senior Editor of *Journal of Chemical Dependency Treatment.*

Foreword

I am truly honored to have been asked to write the foreword for this special volume on women. The articles in this publication are written by women who have dedicated their lives to improving the quality and availability of alcoholism and drug addictions treatment for women in the United States. As I read the work presented here, I was reminded of the power, richness and diversity that is characteristic of the hundreds of advocates for women's services I have gotten to know and love over the past twenty years. The range of issues covered, from treating chemically dependent lesbians and bisexual women, to using the relational model as a context for treatment, to the role of culture in treatment services and treatment effectiveness, reflect incredible progress and advancements in our understanding of successful therapeutic models that assist women with alcoholism and drug addictions to begin and sustain recovery. It is wonderful to have this opportunity to read the work in this volume and reflect on our progress, especially at a time when so many of the gains we have made in treating women are threatened.

Twenty-five years ago, there was almost no gender specific treatment in this country. In fact, if you suggested that women might require services that were different from men, you were often ridiculed and isolated as a crazy fringe element. This is obviously no longer the case. While the stigma associated with alcoholism and drug addiction among women has not evaporated, even among treatment professionals in the field, the times are radically different.

Today, there are hundreds of programs for women across the

[Haworth co-indexing entry note]: "Foreword." Galbraith, Susan. Co-published simultaneously in *Journal of Chemical Dependency Treatment* (The Haworth Press, Inc.) Vol. 6, No. 1/2, 1996, pp. xiii-xv; and: *Chemical Dependency: Women at Risk* (ed: Brenda L. Underhill, and Dana G. Finnegan) The Haworth Press, Inc., 1996, pp. xiii-xv; and: *Chemical Dependency: Women at Risk* (ed: Brenda L. Underhill, and Dana G. Finnegan) Harrington Park Press, an imprint of The Haworth Press, Inc., 1996, pp. xiii-xv. Single or multiple copies of this article are available from The Haworth Document Delivery Service [1-800-342-9678, 9:00 a.m. - 5:00 p.m. (EST) E-mail address: getinfo@haworth.com].

xiii

country. Many of these programs are providing comprehensive and gender specific services for women, their partners, and their families. Programs are providing treatment by and for women in loving and supportive environments where women can get clean and sober, deal with the toll addiction has taken, and rebuild healthy and meaningful lives.

The articles in this collection reflect how much we have learned. We have learned how to break down the barriers that stand in the way of women entering treatment and know what the treatment experience must include once a woman gets there. We have learned that many women enter treatment with long and devastating histories of sexual and physical abuse and need support in integrating these past experiences in order to stay clean and sober. We have learned that culture does make a difference in how women internalize their feelings about addiction and what they need to move forward. We have adopted the work of leading feminist thinkers, especially from the Stone Center at Wellesley College where the relational model discussed in a number of articles here first originated. In short, we have changed the nature of addictions treatment by pushing the boundaries of conventional wisdom and trusting our instincts about the power of trust, identity, and relationships.

The success of these efforts is reflected throughout the writings in this volume. Each article provides some of the best thinking about the challenges of designing and implementing gender specific and culturally relevant treatment.

As I read these articles, I was struck again by how challenging and difficult it will be in the current political and economic climate to sustain the progress we have made and implement the fine recommendations presented here. Federal and state support for alcoholism and drug addictions treatment is being cut dramatically. In this year alone, we face the loss of over five hundred million dollars in federal funding for treatment, prevention and education services. At the same time, the Medicaid program is being cut and sent to the states in block grants. States are transforming their Medicaid programs by moving individuals into managed care systems that provide minimal addictions treatment services. And, support for a comprehensive treatment benefit through private insurers is a phenomenon of the past. It's hard to believe that just one year ago, four separate

Congressional committees included comprehensive drug and alcohol treatment benefits in their health care reform proposals. The public policy on this issue has deteriorated with rapid speed.

There is also a reemergence of a moralistic view of addictions and an increase in "blaming the victim" rhetoric. Congress is moving rapidly to eliminate SSI benefits for individuals who are disabled as a result of their addictions. With the loss of this entitlement will also go Medicaid and access to health care and treatment services. There is also a lot of mean talk about cutting benefits to women on AFDC who are alcoholic and drug dependent with very little emphasis on the importance of treatment in increasing self-sufficiency. Finally, there are rumblings everywhere about poor women who use drugs during pregnancy and recommendations for swift and harsh punishment.

We're in an uphill battle to sustain the gains made in women's treatment services in this country over the past twenty years. In fact, it is going to take everything we've got. Programs are closing and there are likely to be many more to follow. There is nothing, however, that can take away the knowledge we have gained about what works for women and the successes of our struggle to create safe places where women can meet, talk and support each other in recovery. This is nowhere more evident to me than in the time I spend each week with women in recovery who are incarcerated at the prison in my area. Women at the prison are living in the most extreme conditions of isolation and deprivation. Even so, each week our group meets and creates an environment of support, love and hope for the future. Nothing is more powerful than the spirit of the women gathered together to support each other in recovery.

Susan Galbraith
Washington, DC

Preface

The field of chemical dependency has indeed made significant strides in the past twenty-five years in our understanding of women, addiction and recovery. The transformations inherent in the conceptual framework shift from "an alcoholic (addict) is an alcoholic (addict)" to understanding that addiction is a complex bio-psycho-social-spiritual disease which occurs in the context of women's lives, are reflected in this creative and thought-provoking collection of articles. The authors represent a wide variety of training and experience, including professionals who come from research, prevention, treatment community organizing and policy-making backgrounds.

In her exploratory study, Laurie Drabble examines the key service elements of effective residential recovery services for alcoholic women. In addition to identifying general themes which emerged from her data, Drabble also summarizes the policy and service delivery implications of her study for women's treatment. Her article places women's alcohol and drug treatment services in a historical context as she provides a comprehensive search of the literature on women's needs in treatment and the barriers to treatment which result in women continuing to be an underserved population.

The next two articles apply the work of the Stone Center for Developmental Studies at Wellesley College on the use of the relational model in treating chemically dependent women. Norma Finkelstein in her article, "Using the Relational Model as a Context for Treating Pregnant and Parenting Chemically Dependent Women," offers a theoretical model, adapted from the self-in-relation model,

[Haworth co-indexing entry note]: "Preface." Underhill, Brenda L. Co-published simultaneously in *Journal of Chemical Dependency Treatment* (The Haworth Press, Inc.) Vol. 6, No. 1/2, 1996, pp. xvii-xix; and: *Chemical Dependency: Women at Risk* (ed: Brenda L. Underhill, and Dana G. Finnegan) The Haworth Press, Inc., 1996, pp. xvii-xix; and: *Chemical Dependency: Women at Risk* (ed: Brenda L. Underhill, and Dana G. Finnegan) Harrington Park Press, an imprint of The Haworth Press, Inc., 1996, pp. xvii-xix. Single or multiple copies of this article are available from The Haworth Document Delivery Service [1-800-342-9678, 9:00 a.m. - 5:00 p.m. (EST) E-mail address: getinfo@haworth.com].

which aids in understanding women's lives both from a multi-generational and lifespan perspective. Special consideration is given to issues of sexuality, violence and sexual abuse, codependence and parenting.

Similarly, Patricia Cawley and Laurie Markoff explore the effects on client retention of the relational model of multi-systems case management. One particular program, Project Second Beginning, is described in detail, using the clinical examples to more clearly delineate the implementation of this model in the treatment of women's chemical dependency. The importance of relationships among staff as sources of support, personal and professional growth and the prevention of burnout is also discussed within the context of the relational model. In addition, both of these articles explore a central contradiction of society's expectations of women, i.e., how to promote the recovery of women both as individuals and as parents.

In keeping with the understanding that women are not a homogeneous group, with "one size fits all" treatment, Carmella Woll discusses the critical role culture plays in the efficacy of treatment. Woll points out our ethical responsibility as service providers to respect cultural and individual differences. A three-stage cultural assessment model is discussed for planning recovery services in order to identify patterns of beliefs and customs that can assist or hinder women in achieving and maintaining recovery.

Dana Finnegan and Emily McNally explore the multiple traumas many lesbian and bisexual women experience in their long-term recovery from addiction, sexism and the devastating effects of societal homophobia and heterosexism. Integrating the trauma work of Judith Herman, Finnegan and McNally describe why so many lesbians and bisexual women with long-term recovery battle with these complex and painful circumstances; how they do so; and what life and treatment strategies may assist them in their recovery. The authors also discuss the essential treatment responsibilities of therapists engaged in this work

In "HIV, Women and Alcohol Recovery: Risks, Reality and Responses" presented by Benson, Quackenbush and Haas, the much-neglected topic of the importance of providers addressing HIV with women in recovery is discussed. The authors point out the unique issues women in recovery face in relation to the HIV epidemic, including the limited attention paid to their risks and the more limited range of prevention interventions directed toward women's situations and needs. Five principles are described, applicable to both individual and group work, which assist service providers in establishing a framework for discussions of sexuality and HIV in the context of recovery. The need for providers to assist women in developing their skills in self-advocacy and assertiveness is also discussed.

The final article, "Women's Marijuana Problems: An Overview with Implications for Outreach, Intervention, Treatment, and Research" by Susan Chacín, provides the most comprehensive review of marijuana addiction in women written to date. Specific recommendations for professionals in the areas of outreach, intervention, treatment, and research are discussed in detail.

The seven articles in this special volume are intended to supplement the existing body of knowledge on women and chemical dependency both on a theoretical and practical level. They reflect an increasing awareness of treatment complexities in integrating our understanding of the interplay of the nature of addiction and the psychological and social realities of women's lives. The authors have themselves been involved for many years in changing both our vision and our practice of service delivery to women with alcohol and other drug problems. It is with great appreciation and respect that I present this book.

Sincere appreciation and gratitude is extended to Dr. Dana Finnegan for her patience, persistence and expertise. Special thanks goes to Dr. Margaret Cramer for her assistance and support in completing this volume. Acknowledgement is extended to my colleagues in the field who work every day with commitment, dedication and vision.

These are, indeed, difficult financial times as public funding dwindles and treatment programs scramble to deal with the ramifications of managed care on our industry. However, I sincerely believe that while change is inevitable, we will continue to work together with compassion for the women and children we serve. As treatment professionals, paraprofessionals and volunteers, we will reclaim the "problems" we face in our field as challenges for which solutions can and will be found.

Brenda L. Underhill, MS, CAC

Elements of Effective Services for Women in Recovery: Implications for Clinicians and Program Supervisors

Laurie Drabble, MSW, CADC

SUMMARY. This chapter provides an overview of elements of effective services for women as identified in an exploratory study conducted by the author of this article. Service areas include (1) Medical Care/Health Care Issues; (2) Emotional/Psychosocial Issues; (3) Life Skills; (4) Partner and Parenting Issues and (5) Culturally Specific/Population Specific Services. General themes that emerged in the research project and implications for providers of alcohol recovery services are discussed. *[Article copies available from The Haworth Document Delivery Service: 1-800-342-9678. E-mail address: getinfo@haworth.com]*

Before the emergence of the women's movement, female alcohol and drug dependency was generally regarded as an uncommon

Laurie Drabble is an organizational consultant and former Executive Director of the California Women's Commission on Alcohol and Drug Dependencies. She serves as Chair of the Women's Health Council, a statewide advisory body for the California Department of Human Services, Office of Women's Health and Vice-Chair of the Women's Constituent Committee with the California Department of Alcohol and Drug Programs. In addition, Laurie is currently pursuing a doctorate degree at the U.C. Berkeley of Social Welfare.

[Haworth co-indexing entry note]: "Elements of Effective Services for Women in Recovery: Implications for Clinicians and Program Supervisors." Drabble, Laurie. Co-published simultaneously in *Journal of Chemical Dependency Treatment* (The Haworth Press, Inc.) Vol. 6, No. 1/2, 1996, pp. 1-21; and: *Chemical Dependency: Women at Risk* (ed: Brenda L. Underhill, and Dana G. Finnegan) The Haworth Press, Inc., 1996, pp. 1-21; and: *Chemical Dependency: Women at Risk* (ed: Brenda L. Underhill, and Dana G. Finnegan) Harrington Park Press, an imprint of The Haworth Press, Inc., 1996, pp. 1-21. Single or multiple copies of this article are available from The Haworth Document Delivery Service [1-800-342-9678, 9:00 a.m. - 5:00 p.m. (EST) E-mail address: getinfo@haworth.com].

manifestation of a basically masculine disease; as a result, it was often overlooked, underreported, underdiagnosed, and undertreated (Bell Unger, 1988). In the 1970s, largely as a result of advocacy by feminists and the influence of the women's movement, interest in research, treatment needs and prevention strategies of alcoholic and drug dependent women increased.

In spite of the progress that has been made in the last 20 years, however, women have remained underserved in treatment and recovery programs. Alcoholic women are still stigmatized and pathologized for their addiction. For example, Waisberg and Page (1988) found that clinicians perceived female patients with "masculine" symptoms like alcoholism or antisocial behavior to be more psychologically disturbed than male patients with the same symptoms. In addition, women are often inappropriately served. Most alcohol and drug programs are still designed by and for men, and are based on a male model of treatment (Roth, 1991; Mondanaro, 1989). Though programs designed to meet the specific needs of women have had considerable success (Beckman and Amaro, 1984; Dahlgren and Willander, 1989; NCA, 1987), many providers of recovery services fail to take advantage of the growing body of research and experiential knowledge that offers direction for the provision of services that are truly effective for women.

The author of this article conducted an exploratory study on elements of effective residential recovery services for alcoholic women. The primary purpose of the study was to identify core services that, based on the experience of a diverse sample of fifteen experts in the provision of services to alcohol and drug dependent women, should be considered "minimum" or basic to addressing the needs of women clients. Experts in the study were selected based on their experience in the design, administration, and delivery of services for women and on their experience in working with women from diverse ethnic and cultural backgrounds. They were given an opportunity to review a checklist of 105 possible program elements developed from an extensive review of relevant literature and categorize them into mandatory/minimum, desirable and ideal services. Although the focus of the study was on residential services for alcoholic women, it is anticipated that findings will be of value in diverse settings with both alcohol and drug dependent women. The collective wisdom and experience reflected in the results of the study have important implications for all clinicians and program supervisors working with alcohol and drug dependent women.

ELEMENTS OF EFFECTIVE SERVICES

The literature on the treatment needs of women alcoholics identifies a wide range of issues that need to be addressed in recovery (Beckman, 1984; Finkelstein and others, 1990; Glover-Reed, Beschner and Mondanaro, 1981, 1982; Lemay, 1980; Lester, 1982; Mondanaro, 1981; Nespor, 1990; Roman, 1988; Roth, 1991, 1991a; Turnbull, 1989; Wilsnack and Beckman, 1984; Women's Alcoholism Center, 1990). The broad areas revealed in the literature and integrated into the study questionnaire include medical/health care needs, emotional/psychosocial issues, life skills, and partner and parenting issues. In addition, the literature identifies particular issues and corresponding treatment needs of women from specific populations and from diverse cultural backgrounds (Brisbane and Womble, 1986; Dawkins and Harper, 1983; LaDue, 1991; Mora, 1990; Mora and Gilbert, 1991; Sun, 1991; Taha-Cisse, 1991; Underhill and Ostermann, 1991; Weibel-Orlando, 1986), including African American women, Asian American women, Latinas, Native American women, and lesbians. (See Figure 1.)

Medical Care/Health Care Issues

Alcohol and other drugs often impact the bodies and overall health of women differently than that of men. Women become intoxicated after drinking smaller quantities of alcohol than are needed to create intoxication among men (NIAAA, 1990) and women show a shorter average duration of excessive drinking before suffering negative health consequences (Hill, 1984, 1986). Compared to other women, heavy drinking women and alcoholic women frequently have more gynecological and obstetrical problems (Johnson, 1991; NIAAA, 1990; Roman, 1988) and may be at higher risk for HIV/AIDS. Fetal alcohol syndrome (FAS) is one of

FIGURE 1. Elements of Effective Programs for Residential Alcohol Recovery Programs Serving Women: Minimum Program Elements

HEALTH ISSUES

General Health, Reproductive Health, HIV/AIDS

Educational components in program on HIV/AIDS and transmission prevention.

Referral to anonymous or confidential test sites that provide pre/post test counseling for HIV/AIDS. (Anonymous sites strongly preferred)

Referral to agencies and support groups providing services for women who are HIV positive.

Educational components on reproductive health during program stay.

Educational components on Fetal Alcohol Syndrome and Fetal Alcohol Effects (accompanied by support to counter potential parental guilt and shame issues).

Health survey form, referral to a local clinic for a medical exam as needed.

Health Promotion

Referral to smoking cessation resources and limitations on smoking areas.

Educational components about the physical effects of alcohol and other drug use.

Education about prescription and over the counter drugs.

Access to written materials and referrals for health maintenance including self breast exam and obtaining gynecological exams.

Structured physical recreational activities.

Supervision of residents in relation to meal preparation and nutrition.

Education about health maintenance including self breast exam and obtaining gynecological exams.

PSYCHOSOCIAL ISSUES

Self-Esteem/Shame Issues

Structured women's groups that address issues of self-esteem, guilt and shame.

Utilization of women staff as role models. Stress and crisis management skill-building.

Community education about women's alcohol and drug issues to increase public awareness and reduce stigma.

Use of supportive counseling and avoidance of extremely confrontational counseling styles.

Victimization Issues

Linkages to agencies/experts in community in relation to domestic violence, rape, childhood abuse.

Written policies that ensure protection of participants in relation to sexual harassment and sexual advances from staff.

Victimization Issues, continued

Assessment of victimization issues within intake process.

Educational sessions on the dynamics of domestic violence.

Familial Alcohol/Drug Dependence

Program exit planning in relation to living arrangements or interactions involving practicing alcoholics or addicts.

Education about alcoholic family dynamics.

Co-existing problems/disorders

Procedures for referrals to psychological resources.

Educational components on illegal/legal drug use, depression and eating disorders.

Assessment or questions on intake related to other drug use including prescription drug use, individual or familial history of depression and eating disorders.

Issues related to Sexuality

Referral procedures for linking participants to lesbian/gay community support agencies or social networks.

Use of educational materials and program content that does not presume participant heterosexuality.

Educational sessions on setting sexual limits and skills for practicing "safer" sex.

Access to low literacy educational material on sex, sexuality (including bi-sexuality and lesbianism) and "safer" sex practices.

Educational sessions on basic information about sexuality (including information about sexual orientation).

PARTNER AND PARENTING ISSUES

Partner/Family issues

Agency policy, procedures and practices that support participants to identify and utilize alternative support networks and non-traditional "families."

Groups and educational sessions for participants on dealing with partner and family issues in recovery.

Educational sessions on healthy relationships with partners.

Parenting Issues

Clear procedures on reporting suspected child abuse.

Referral to community based agencies offering parenting skills. Special support group sessions for parenting women in recovery.

Support activities (group or individual) for women who have had their children removed, whose children are in foster care, or who choose not to parent their children.

LIFE SKILLS

Vocational Rehabilitation

Referral to vocational rehabilitation services and local job training programs.

Referral to job seeking/job readiness programs.

Referral to literacy programs as needed.

Linkage to programs offering GED.

Referral to local colleges and trade schools.

Social Networks

Group outings to community based self-help meetings.

Required group social/recreational activities.

Communication Skills

Referral to community based resources on building communication skills as needed.

Accessing Support Services

Referral to other social service agencies as needed.

Referral to housing resources.

Referral to legal assistance as needed.

Groups and/or individual support for exit planning.

Assistance in planning for transportation/assistance with navigating public transportation systems.

Procedures for organizational linkages with staff of allied agencies including social services, parole or probation

PROVISION OF SERVICES TO DIVERSE POPULATIONS OF WOMEN

Training for staff and management on working in and running multi-cultural organizations.

Training for staff in addressing racism, homophobia, ageism, and able-bodyism.

Support for participation in culturally relevant community activities and self-help groups.

Outreach for staff through publications and organizations that reach women of color, lesbians, women with disabilities and older women.

Attention to the creation of an environment that reflects diverse populations of women including pictures, posters, and inclusive educational reading material, videos, and films.

Written commitment to agency management and board of directors that is reflective of the population the program plans to serve.

Written policy to promote that staff composition be reflective of the population that the program plans to serve.

Extensive outreach for hiring new staff including "non-traditional" outreach methods like word of mouth.

Extensive outreach for hiring new staff including "non-traditional" outreach methods like word of mouth.

Ensuring participant access to bi-lingual, bi-cultural staff.

Integration of diverse cultural celebrations into program activities.

Conducting women of color support groups.

Accessible Services

Education of staff on diverse disabilities and on maintaining an "attitudinal" accessible program.

Maintain procedures for access to sign language interpreters.

Ensure development and maintenance of a site that is physically accessible.

Programs Serving a Specific Population

Ensure that staff and program are culturally-sensitive (respect for

traditions, values and spiritual beliefs).

Ensure that staff and program are culturally-relevant (understand the expectations and needs of the program participant).

Ensure that the program is an active, visible part of the community being served

Hire staff that reflect the language and culture/s of the community to be served.

Conduct outreach that is specific to a given community.

Ensure that staff and program are culturally-competent (beyond having staff with a background from a given culture/population— have staff that have extensive knowledge of the culture and language of a given community).

Ensure that program development and implementation is conducted by and for the population to be served.

the top three known causes of birth defects, with accompanying mental retardation and the only preventable cause among those three (NCADD, 1990). The mortality rate of women with alcohol problems is also equal to or greater than that of alcoholic men and non-alcoholic women (Blume, 1986, 1986a, 1987; NIAAA, 1990).

In general, study respondents tended to identify linkages with off-site medical health care resources and education on health issues as a basic, minimum program requirement for serving women. Referral to HIV/AIDS test sites and to agencies providing support to HIV positive women were overwhelmingly identified as minimum requirements by fourteen respondents. However, several respondents felt that referral to anonymous test sites was either essential or strongly preferable to referral to confidential test sites. The provision of educational components on HIV/AIDS was identified by all fifteen respondents as a minimum program element. (Only two other out of 105 specific program elements received full consensus from respondents as minimum program elements). Education on reproductive health and Fetal Alcohol Syndrome (FAS) and Fetal Alcohol Effects (FAE) were identified by thirteen and twelve respondents respectively. In relation to education on FAS/FAE, two respondents stressed that it was important that qualified staff be available to address issues of fear, guilt, and shame which may surface for alcoholic women who are parents.

A significant majority (ten or more of fifteen respondents) identified the following health promotion activities as minimum program elements for women: educational components on the effects of alcohol and other drugs, including prescription and over-the-counter drugs; access to written materials and referrals for health maintenance, including self breast exam and obtaining gynecological services; and referral to smoking cessation resources and limitations on smoking areas.

Emotional/Psychosocial Issues

There are a number of psychosocial issues correlated with alcoholism among women that differ from those of men. The reality of sexism, experiences of violence and abuse, and imposition of different social expectations for women and men are all important parts of the environment that surround alcoholism and alcohol-related problems among women. Some of the issues include internalization of stigma, victimization issues, familial/partner issues, sexuality, and co-existing disorders.

Most of the program elements outlined in this section were rated by a significant majority of respondents as minimum program elements. However, several program elements were given mixed reviews by respondents. Respondents tended to feel that counselors should have the capacity to deal with multiple emotional/ psychosocial issues when and if they arise, but that program participants should not be "pushed," especially women in early recovery.

Self Esteem/Shame Issues. In comparison to alcoholic men and non-alcoholic women, alcoholic women often exhibit more feelings of fear, guilt, and shame (Gomberg, 1987). Elements of residential recovery services for women that were perceived as fundamental for enhancing the self-esteem of women alcoholics by ten or more of the respondents, included the provision of structured women's groups to address issues of self-esteem, guilt, and shame; utilization of women staff as role models; and stress and crisis management skill building. In addition, twelve respondents felt that minimum program elements for women should extend beyond the focus on individual alcoholics to provide community education on alcohol and drug issues among women in an attempt to increase awareness and reduce stigma. Ten respondents advocated use of supportive counseling and avoidance of extremely confrontational counseling methods. They felt that tactics used in some drug recovery programs which involve trying to "break down" or humiliate participants as part of the therapeutic process were counterproductive for women alcoholics or addicts whose self-esteem is already fragile.

Victimization Issues. Women in recovery are frequently survivors of childhood sexual abuse (with studies reporting from 34 to 75 percent) (Russell and Wilsnack, 1991) and often have higher levels of domestic violence in their backgrounds (Miller, Downs and Gondoli, 1989). In discussion, most of the respondents believed that program elements need to acknowledge, recognize, and, to a limited degree, address victimization issues, but that the primary focus of the residential recovery program should be on establishing a foundation of sobriety. Respondents, regardless of the category they selected for these elements, tended to support the implementation of some programmatic resources for dealing with victimization issues with the stipulation that such services be based on the need and the "timing" of individual participants. Finally, fourteen respondents believed that programs should have written policies that ensure protection of participants in relation to sexual harassment and sexual advances from staff. In relation to this last issue, one respondent stated that "one of the worst forms of abuse is when therapists or counselors are unwilling to maintain professional behavior with participants."

Familial Alcohol and Drug Dependence. Children of alcoholics are more likely than children from non-alcoholic families to develop alcoholism as adults and to find themselves in adult relationships with an alcoholic partner (Black, 1986; Gomberg, Nelson and Hatchett, 1991). Respondents believed that education about alcoholic family dynamics and exit planning in relation to living arrangements or interactions involving practicing alcoholics or addicts should be a minimum program requirement. Process groups for daughters of alcoholics received mixed results. Participants felt that such program content might be useful (even critical) for some clients, but that, in their experience, dealing with these issues in depth during early recovery could be counterproductive for others.

Issues Related to Sexuality. Covington (1985) identifies several reasons for examining the relationship between alcohol and sexuality. First, there is a popular misperception that alcohol is an aphrodisiac. Second, heavy drinking and alcoholism may be directly related to sexual dysfunctions. Third, two major problems in recovery from alcoholism are family relationships and difficulties in sexual functioning. Some disorders or problems addressed most frequently in reviews of the literature on women's alcohol problems include depression or other psychiatric problems, poly drug abuse and prescription drug abuse, and eating disorders (NIAAA, 1991).

Elements in this category received a great deal of support as minimum program elements. Fourteen out of fifteen respondents believed that minimum program elements should include provision of educational sessions on setting sexual limits and skills for practicing "safer sex," referral procedures for linking participants to lesbian/gay community support agencies or social networks, and use of educational content and materials that do not presume participant heterosexuality. Respondents also generally supported access to low literacy educational materials and provision of educational sessions on sex and sexuality. Some respondents felt that access to openly lesbian staff might not be possible or necessary in some programs, hence it was not identified as a minimum program element. However, it is worth noting that lesbian respondents tended to feel that this element, in addition to the others above, were all necessary to counter homophobia in programs and to support lesbian/bisexual participants. One respondent commented that it was not enough to address the needs of lesbian participants, but that the discomfort of heterosexual women around lesbianism needed to be addressed with sensitivity.

Co-existing Problems/Disorders. Consistent with the results above, in relation to minimum program elements, respondents favored addressing co-existing disorders like other drug use, depression, or eating disorders through assessment, education, and referral. On-site psychological counseling for depression or eating disorders was perceived largely as optimal or desirable, but in two cases, as not needed. Perception of the importance of educational sessions on body image and the impact of social expectations of women in relation to size and appearance were mostly divided between minimum and desirable categories. One respondent pointed out that clinical depression is different from the kind of depression often resulting from problem drinking. She commented that alcoholic women are often misdiagnosed with depression and that program staff need to pay attention to participant mood and behavior as they evolve in the process of early recovery.

Life Skills

Many women in recovery from alcohol related problems face challenges in relation to developing the life skills needed to build and maintain a foundation for surviving and thriving in recovery. Such life skills include the development of vocational skills, social networks, communication and relational skills, and basic survival skills (Gomberg, 1986; Finkelstein and others, 1990; Women's Alcoholism Center, 1990). Study participants consistently placed a high value on linking participants to community based resources for job training, job readiness, education, and enhancing communication skills. On-site services related to vocational and communication skills were generally perceived as desirable or optimal, depending on program and community resources. All fifteen respondents seemed to feel that assisting participants to access support services and to utilize support networks were important minimum program elements.

Partner and Parenting Issues

Respondents tended to identify educational sessions and group counseling around partner and parenting issues as minimum program elements for women. In addition, participants tended to urge linkage of participants and their families to outside resources. Respondents unanimously identified the need for clear procedures on reporting suspected child abuse to be critical for any recovery program.

In terms of family issues, respondents emphasized the need of support for women to discuss, assess, and learn about their relationships in the context of the program. Some felt that having services for partners and family members would be valuable, but that limited resources would make this program "desirable" or "optimal." Some of the respondents pointed out that, unfortunately, by the time women reach treatment they often have no support or are with partners who may be unwilling to participate in a family recovery process.

During the interviews, most participants (eight) said that having some kind of resources for pregnant women and women with children was important. In general, the predominant themes related to parenting in discussions were that (1) women with children should have accessible and acceptable treatment resources; (2) women who are not pregnant or parenting, or who choose not to be with their children in recovery, should also have access to treatment; (3) treatment services and staff should respect and provide support to women regardless of their reproductive choices; (4) the issues of women who have lost or given up custody of their children should also be addressed in recovery; and (5) treatment delivery systems should operate on the assumption that recovery services that benefit women are also beneficial to their children and should not foster the impression that there is an inherently adversarial relationship between alcohol dependent women and their children or fetuses.

Culturally Specific/Population Specific Services

Participants affirmed the claims of the literature in relation to the differing needs of various populations of women (Brisbane and Womble, 1986; Dawkins and Harper, 1983; LaDue, 1991; Mora, 1990; Mora and Gilbert, 1991; Sun, 1991; Taha-Cisse, 1991; Underhill and Ostermann, 1991; Weibel-Orlando, 1986). Respondents, overall, placed a high value on the provision of services which would meet the needs of diverse or specific populations of women. In general, respondents felt that it was important that residential programs for women be capable of serving a multicultural population. In addition, respondents believed it was necessary to develop culturally specific services for populations of women who may not be comfortable or likely to access "general" programs. For example, one respondent stated that Native American women (who are vastly under-served) in their community would not participate in a program which did not reflect their own cultural and spiritual values and that it was critical that Native American services be delivered by Native Americans. Most respondents felt that it was important for women to have the choice to access both multi-cultural programs and culturally-specific programs based on their individual needs and preferences. Similar values were reflected in relation to serving lesbians and bisexual women. The development of services for women with different disabilities that are accessible, physically and in relation to clinician/staff attitude, were also considered fundamental.

All but two of the program elements listed in this section were identified by at least ten of the fifteen respondents as minimum program requirements. Some of the elements identified in this section as minimum received qualifying comments from a number of respondents. For example, two respondents felt that women of color support groups may not be appropriate to every program, that such groups might depend on the demographics of the program, the skill of the staff, and an assessment of whether it is appropriate to "lump together" diverse populations of women under one "women of color" umbrella.

Barriers to Implementing Effective Services for Women

Women often face a range of structural, personal, and environmental barriers to recovery. For example, women are more likely to encounter opposition to treatment from family and friends (Beckman, 1984). Women are also more likely to face barriers to treatment as primary caretakers of children because of the scarcity of programs serving women with children or offering childcare alternatives (Finkelstein, 1991; Reckman, Babcock and O'Bryan, 1984). Study participants, in interviews, identified a wide range of barriers that, in their experience, are frequently faced by women in need of treatment. (The most frequently discussed barriers are outlined in Figure 2.)

GENERAL THEMES

There were a number of themes which emerged in the process of analyzing data from this study. These are delineated and discussed here.

1. Respect for the Distinct Recovery Needs of Women Alcoholics

Respondents unanimously concurred with the literature in reiterating the fact that the experience of alcoholism and the recovery needs of women are significantly different from those of men (Beckman, 1984; Finkelstein and others, 1990; Glover-Reed, Beschner and Mondanaro, 1981; Roman, 1988; Roth, 1991; Wilsnack and Beckman, 1984). Participants strongly support the design and implementation of women-specific services. As one respondent commented after a lengthy discussion of the outlined program elements: "Women's services are not just men's services with tampons." Clinicians must be versed in the specific needs that arise for women in various phases of recovery. In addition, clinicians must be prepared to take on a number of roles in identifying appropriate interventions for women: therapist, educator, broker of ancillary services and advocate.

FIGURE 2. Barriers to the Delivery of Effective Services for Alcoholic Women

INDIVIDUAL BARRIERS
Personal denial among alcoholic women.

ENVIRONMENTAL BARRIERS
Stigma attached to women with alcohol problems.

Similar denial on the part of family members and helping professionals.

Additional stigma and public hostility toward pregnant or parenting alcoholics.

Lack of family support for identification of alcohol problems and for seeking treatment/recovery services.

Lack of a range of available and acceptable childcare alternatives. Unconscious sexism on the part of staff.

Limited economic resources. Women usually earn less than men and have less access to insurance.

Ignorance of program staff about women's issues.

Problems with access to safe, affordable transportation.

Shortage of population and culturally specific programs for women.

Perceived responsibility for partners.

Relative lack of research about women's alcohol problems and recovery needs.

Experiences of oppression (e.g., based on race, ethnicity, sex or sexual orientation) both real and internalized.

Public/neighborhood resistance to welcoming programs for women.

Lack of information about where or how to obtain services.

Failure of funding sources and programs to pursue multiple funding sources.

Co-dependence or involvement in alcohol abusing relationships/support networks.

Difficulty in fundraising for women-specific services.

Lack of self-esteem and a sense of "deserving" a better, sober life.

Failure of programs to "match" participants/clients to programs that best meet their needs and preferences.

2. Dealing with Multiple Issues in Recovery

One area that generated a great deal of discussion was related to assisting women to deal with multiple issues in recovery. The literature identifies a wide range of issues common to women in recovery (Gomberg, 1986; Finkelstein and others, 1990; Glover-Reed, Beschner and Mondanaro, 1981; NCADD, 1990; Roman, 1988; Roth, 1991;

Wilsnack and Beckman, 1984; Women's Alcoholism Center, 1990). A significant number of respondents expressed both enthusiastic support for serious concern about addressing issues beyond basic recovery, from smoking cessation to dealing with childhood victimization. Even with the different ratings, there was consistency among respondents in two important ways. First, respondents agreed that women faced important multiple issues in recovery and that many of those issues would need to be addressed at some time in the recovery process. Indeed, for many women, addressing a particular issue might be considered critical for the prevention of relapse into active alcoholism. Second, respondents believed that when and how these issues were addressed had to be handled with sensitivity in program design and by program staff. The sentiment appeared to be that programs and clinicians should have resources for dealing with multiple issues but should not, by design, "overwhelm" participants in early recovery. Third, respondents who discussed these issues tended to support the principle that the "timing" for addressing the issues had to be determined based on the needs and the preferences of an individual woman in recovery, that there was no universal "right time" to address particular issues.

3. Access to Additional Services for Recovering Women

A related theme was the need for linkages to a wide range of supporting and ancillary services in each of the areas explored as discussed by Glover Reed (1987). Although there was some variation among participants in relation to whether a particular service should be available on site or through referral to community resources, there was universal agreement for the need to provide participants with the resources to address their issues or skill deficits.

4. The Importance of Culturally and Population Specific Services

Study respondents tended to actively support the value of programs designed to meet the needs of diverse women. Many of the respondents gave voice to the specific concerns of the underserved populations they represent or work with. Regardless of their particular "constituent" group, respondents placed a high value on both multicultural programs accessible to women of diverse cultures and populations, and the development of culturally specific and population specific programs that may be able to reach women when the "general" programs may not. In addition, respondents overall favored training for working with diverse populations of women, instituting measures to assure diverse staff composition and creating environments and linkages that support participant cultural identities.

5. The Importance of Empowerment

Respondents tended to identify the concept of empowerment as critical to the recovering individual as well as important to the philosophical basis and design of programs. There was significant support for this concept as in the section of the questionnaire related to feminist principle (Van den Bergh, 1986, 1991) in the delivery of services. However, the theme of empowerment was also raised in relation to each of the larger program element groupings by one respondent or another during the course of the interviews. The commitment to the individual and collective empowerment of women appeared to be a fundamental criteria guiding respondents' evaluation of the utility of different program elements as well as a driving force behind their dedication to their own work.

CONCLUSION

Several implications for planners, administrators and providers of alcohol recovery services may be summarized from the results of this study. These are delineated below.

1. When starting new services for women, it is preferable that they be women only and women specific in design.
2. Co-gender agencies should create women's specific programs.
3. Programs serving women should integrate program elements that address women's health issues, emotional/psychosocial issues, life skills, and parenting and partner issues.
4. The design of programs should account for the diverse needs of different cultural groups and specific sub-populations of women.

5. Communities should try to ensure that women have access to both multicultural and culturally/population specific program resources.
6. All programs serving women should ensure that staff are adequately trained in relation to alcoholism in women and the multiple needs of women in recovery.
7. All programs serving women should ensure that they have extensive linkages and resources in relation to dealing with the wide range of needs women may have in relation to their efforts to survive, recover, and thrive.
8. Programs should assess their written policies in relation to their commitment to hiring diverse staff who are representative of the women they serve.
9. Programs should explore and implement creative strategies to reach out to women who might not otherwise access services.
10. Programs, service providers and participants should all find a role in fighting the stigma attached to alcoholic women and in advocating for increased funding for women's services.
11. Programs, service providers and participants should also take a leadership role in framing the political philosophies and funding priorities in relation to the creation of new funding for both pregnant/parenting women and women in general.
12. Programs should place a high value on the empowerment of women in their programs, on their staff, and in their communities.

REFERENCES

Beckman, L.J. (1984). Treatment needs of women alcoholics. *Alcoholism Treatment Quarterly, 1*(2), 101-113.

Beckman, L.J., & Amaro, H. (1984). Patterns of women's use of alcohol treatment agencies. In S.C. Wilsnack, & L.J. Beckman (Eds.), *Alcohol problems in women* (pp. 349-368). New York: Guilford Press.

Bell Unger, K. (1988). Chemical dependency in women: Meeting the challenges of accurate diagnosis and effective treatment. *Women and Medicine, 149*, 746-750.

Black, C., Bucky, S.F., & Wilder-Padilla, S. (1986). The interpersonal and emotional consequences of being an adult child of an alcoholic parent. *International Journal of the Addictions, 21*(2), 213-231.

Blume, S. (1986). Women and alcohol: A review. *Journal of the American Medical Association, 256*, 1467-1470.

Blume, S.B. (1987). Alcoholism and women's health. In Public Health Services' *Public health reports supplement to the July-August 1987 issue: National conference on women's health* (PHS Pub. No. PHS 86-50193). Washington DC: Department of Health and Human Services.

Brisbane, F.L., & Womble, M. (1986). Afterthoughts and recommendations. Special issue: Treatment of Black alcoholics. *Alcoholism Treatment Quarterly,* 2(3-4), 249-270.

Covington, S. (1985). Chemically dependent women and sexuality. In *Women and addiction: A collection of papers* by Stephanie S. Covington, PhD (pp. 27-45). La Jolla, CA: Author.

Dahlgren, L., & Willander, A. (1989). Are special treatment facilities for female alcoholics needed? *Alcoholism: Clinical and Experimental Research 13,* 499-504.

Dawkins, M.P., & Harper, F.D. (1983). Alcoholism among women: A comparison of black and white problem drinkers. *International Journal of the Addictions, 18,* 333-349.

Finkelstein, N., Duncan, F.A., Derman, L., & Smeltz, J. (1990). *Getting sober, getting well: A treatment guide for caregivers who work with women.* Cambridge, MA: Women's Alcoholism Program of CASPAR.

Finkelstein, N., & Derman, L. (1991). Single-parent women: What a mother can do. In P. Roth (Ed.), *Alcohol and drugs are women's issues, volume one: A review of the issues* (pp. 78-84). New York: Women's Action Alliance and Scarecrow Press.

Glover Reed, B. (1987). Developing women-sensitive drug dependence treatment services: Why so difficult? *Journal of Psychoactive Drugs, 19*(2) 151-164.

Glover Reed, B., Beschner, G.M., & Mondanaro, J. (1981). *Treatment services for drug dependent women: Vol I and II.* Rockville, MD: DHHS Public Health Service.

Gomberg, E.S.L. (1986). Women and alcoholism: Psychosocial issues. In National Institute on Alcohol Abuse and Alcoholism Research Monograph 16, *Women and alcohol: Health related issues* (DHHS Pub. No ADM 96-1139) (pp. 78-120). Rockville, MD: DHHS Public Health Service.

Gomberg, E.S.L. (1987). Shame and guilt issues among women alcoholics. *Alcoholism Treatment Quarterly, 4*(2), 139-155.

Gomberg, E.S.L., Nelson, B.W., & Hatchett, B. (1991). Women, alcoholism and family therapy. *Family Community Health, 13,* 61-71.

Hill, S.Y. (1984). Vulnerability to the biomedical consequences of alcoholism and alcohol-related problems among women. In S. Wilsnack, & L.J. Beckman (Eds.), *Alcohol problems in women* (pp. 121-154). New York: Guilford Press.

Hill, S.Y. (1986). Physiological effects of alcohol in women. In National Institute on Alcohol and Abuse and Alcoholism Monograph No. 16, *Women and alcohol: Health-related issues* (DHHS Pub. No. ADM 86-1139) (pp. 199-214). Rockville MD: U.S. Dept. of Health and Human Services.

Johnson, S. (1991). Recent research: Alcohol and women's bodies. In P. Roth (Ed.), *Alcohol and drugs are women's issues, volume one: A review of the issues* (pp. 32-42). New York: Women's Action Alliance and Scarecrow Press.

LaDue, R.A. (1991). Coyote returns: Survival for Native American women. In P. Roth (Ed.), *Alcohol and drugs are women's issues, volume one: A review of the issues* (pp. 23-31). New York: Women's Action Alliance and Scarecrow Press.

Lemay, D. (1980). The need for awareness of specialized issues in counseling alcoholic women. *Personnel and Guidance Journal, 59*(2), 103-105.

Lester, L. (1982). The special needs of the female alcoholic. *Social Casework: The Journal of Contemporary Social Work, 63*, 451-456.

Miller, B.A., Downs, W.R., & Gondoli, D.M. (1989). Spousal violence among alcoholic women as compared to a random household sample. *Journal of Studies on Alcohol, 50*, 533-540.

Mondanaro, J. (1989). *Chemically dependent women: Assessment and treatment.* Massachusetts: Lexington Books.

Mora, J. (1990). Mexican-American women. In R. Engs (Ed.), *Women: Alcohol and other drugs* (pp. 137-141). Iowa: Kendall/Hunt.

Mora, J., & Gilbert, M.J. (1991). Issues for Latinas: Mexican-American women. In P. Roth (Ed.), *Alcohol and drugs are women's issues, volume one: A review of the issues* (pp. 43-47). New York: Women's Action Alliance and Scarecrow Press.

National Council on Alcoholism. (1987, August). *A federal response to a hidden epidemic: Alcohol and other drug problems among women.* A Report from the National Council on Alcoholism. New York: Author.

National Council on Alcohol and Drug Dependencies. (1990). Fact sheet: Alcoholism, other drug addictions and related problems among women. New York: Author.

National Council on Alcohol and Drug Dependencies. (1990a). Fact sheet: Alcohol-related birth defects. New York: Author.

National Institute on Alcohol Abuse and Alcoholism. (1990, October). Alcohol and Women. Alcohol Alert No. 10. Rockville MD: Author.

National Institute on Alcohol Abuse and Alcoholism. (1991). Alcoholism and Co-existing Disorders. Alcohol Alert No. 14. Rockville, MD: Author

Nespor, K. (1990). Treatment needs of alcohol-dependent women. *International Journal of Psychosomatics, 37*(1-4), 50-52.

Reckman, L.W., Babcock, P., & O'Bryan, T. (1984). Meeting the child care needs of the female alcoholic. *Child Welfare, LXIII*, 541-546.

Roman, P.M. (1988). *Women and alcohol use: A review of the literature.* Rockville, MD: U.S. Department of Health and Human Services.

Roth, P. (Ed). (1991). *Alcohol and drugs are women's issues, volume one: A review of the issues.* New York: Women's Action Alliance and Scarecrow Press.

Russell, S.A., & Wilsnack, S.C. (1991). Adult survivors of childhood sexual abuse: Substance abuse and other consequences. In P. Roth (Ed.), *Alcohol and drugs are women's issues, volume one: A review of the issues* (pp. 61-70). New York: Women's Action Alliance and Scarecrow Press.

Sun, A. (1991). Issues for Asian American women. In P. Roth (Ed.), *Alcohol and drugs are women's issues, volume one: A review of the issues* (pp. 125-129). New York: Women's Action Alliance and Scarecrow Press.

Taha-Cisse, A.H. (1991). Issues for African American women. In P. Roth (Ed.), *Alcohol and drugs are women's issues, volume one: A review of the issues* (pp. 54-60). New York: Women's Action Alliance and Scarecrow Press.

Turnbull, J.E. (1989). Treatment issues for alcoholic women. *Social Casework, 70,* 364-369.

Underhill, B., & Ostermann, S. (1991). The pain of invisibility: Issues for lesbians. In P. Roth (Ed.), *Alcohol and drugs are women's issues, volume one: A review of the issues* (pp. 71-77). New York: Women's Action Alliance and Scarecrow Press.

Van Den Bergh, N. (1991). Having bitten the apple: A feminist perspective on addictions. In N. Van Den Bergh (Ed.), *Feminist perspectives on addictions* (pp. 3-30). New York: Springer Publishing Company.

Waisberg, J., & Page, S. (1988). Gender role nonconformity and perception of mental illness. *Women & Health, 14*(1), 3-16.

Weibel-Orlando, J. (1986). Women and alcohol: Special populations and cross-cultural variations. In National Institute on Alcohol Abuse and Alcoholism Research Monograph 16, *Women and alcohol: Health related issues* (DHHS Pub. No. ADM 96-1139) (pp. 161-187). Rockville, MD: Public Health Service.

Wilsnack, S.C., & Beckman, L.J. (Eds.). (1984). *Alcohol problems in women.* New York: Guilford Press.

Women's Alcoholism Center. (1990). *Raising the roof: Building an alcoholism treatment program for women and children.* San Francisco: Author.

Using the Relational Model as a Context for Treating Pregnant and Parenting Chemically Dependent Women

Norma Finkelstein, PhD

SUMMARY. This article presents a framework for looking at the lives of alcohol and other drug-dependent women within the context of their relationships with others. Included are a presentation of the Self-In-Relation model from the Stone Center for Developmental Studies at Wellesley College and an examination of chemically dependent women from a life-span, relational perspective. *[Article copies available from The Haworth Document Delivery Service: 1-800-342-9678. E-mail address: getinfo@haworth.com].*

THE SELF-RELATION MODEL

In the early 1980s, under the leadership of Dr. Jean Baker Miller, a group of women at the Stone Center for Developmental Studies at

Norma Finkelstein is Director of the Coalition on Addiction, Pregnancy, and Parenting, a state-wide policy, training and service demonstration program in Cambridge, MA. Prior to this, she was Founder and Executive Director of the Women's Alcoholism Program/CASPAR, Inc., a comprehensive prevention, education, and treatment program for chemically dependent women and their families.

This article was adapted from a paper entitled "The Relational Model" in *Pregnancy & Exposure to Alcohol & Other Drug Use,* published by the U.S. Department of Health and Human Services, Substance Abuse and Mental Health Services Administration, Center for Substance Abuse Prevention, July 1993.

[Haworth co-indexing entry note]: "Using the Relational Model as a Context for Treating Pregnant and Parenting Chemically Dependent Women." Finkelstein, Norma. Co-published simultaneously in *Journal of Chemical Dependency Treatment* (The Haworth Press, Inc.) Vol. 6, No. 1/2, 1996, pp. 23-44; and: *Chemical Dependency: Women at Risk* (ed: Brenda L. Underhill, and Dana G. Finnegan) The Haworth Press, Inc., 1996, pp. 23-44; and: *Chemical Dependency: Women at Risk* (ed: Brenda L. Underhill, and Dana G. Finnegan) Harrington Park Press, an imprint of The Haworth Press, Inc., 1996, pp. 23-44. Single or multiple copies of this article are available from The Haworth Document Delivery Service [1-800-342-9678, 9:00 a.m. - 5:00 p.m. (EST) E-mail address: getinfo@haworth.com].

23

Wellesley College began to critique the historical psychoanalytic and developmental theories on women. Their objective has been to discard the universal application of principles of male development in favor of a new conceptual framework and language that will more accurately describe the unique experiences of women.

Traditional theory focuses on autonomy, separation, and development of the "independent" individual. The emphasis has been on self and work rather than on intimacy and love (Gilligan 1982). Theories of healthy male development (which have been portrayed as healthy *human* development) start with the notion that development is based on a person *disconnecting* from relationships. Such theories frequently view relationships as a means to the end of individual achievement. Even the more recent "object relations" theorists posit relationships as being mainly unidirectional and narcissistic.

This clinical stress on individualization is strongly related to Western society's cultural ideals, which assume human separateness. Our culture does not stress attending to interpersonal relationships or empathizing with another's experiences except perhaps in the mother-infant relationship (Miller 1984). Our images of connection are unusually negative and unhealthy, i.e., dependence, weakness, being bound, not free. Dr. Miller defines this as the "deficiency" model of female psychology, which implies that, using standard male models, women see themselves as lacking something, such as a penis or a "separate" sense of self (Jordan 1983).

Dr. Miller first offered her connection-based theory of women's development in 1976. Self-In-Relation theory shifts the emphasis from separation to the "relational self" as the core self-structure in women and as the basis for growth and development (Surrey 1985). Connections are seen as fundamental to psychological growth and healing, including different and new definitions of self, autonomy, and cooperation. Forming and enhancing relationships with others are seen as being central to women's sense of personhood and as critical to a sense of worth, pleasure and effectiveness (Miller 1986).

Theorists at the Stone Center are also examining what kinds of relationships foster growth and empowerment and what distinguishes healthy, growth-producing relationships from unhealthy, destructive ones. Healthy connections are characterized by terms such as "real," "authentic," "dynamic," and "forward-moving." The key is mutuality, where both players have an impact on the connection and each can grow in the relationship. Surrey defines mutually enhancing relationships as those in which persons are involved in mutual processes of engagement, empathy, and empowerment (Surrey 1987).

Dr. Miller has identified five outcomes of growth-enhancing relationships. These are: zest, which includes an increase in feelings of vitality, aliveness, and energy; action, which implies that the relationship empowers an individual to act in the immediate relationship as well as beyond it; greater knowledge of self and others; increased sense of self-worth; and motivation to establish stronger connections (Miller 1986).

Other researchers in addition to the Stone Center have attempted to reexamine life experiences from a female perspective. Gilligan has studied moral development in young women and found that, for them, moral and ethical decisions are embedded within the context of responsibility. In other words, women make moral choices by considering and weighing the interests of all persons involved. Their decisions are thereby contextual in nature. Gilligan characterizes this ideology of care and responsibility as one that recognizes differences in needs and is based on compassion and a belief that no one should be hurt. She contrasts this with a male ideology of rights or justice that is based on "certain truth" and the assumption that everyone, including oneself, should be treated equally (Gilligan 1982). Although, as Gilligan states, the "mature" individual will balance these two approaches, it is the female perspective that has been missing in the literature and research.

> In the portrayal of relationships, women replace the bias of men toward separation with a representation of the inter-dependence of self and other, both in love and in work. By changing the lens of developmental observation from individual achievement to relationships of care, women depict ongoing attachment as the path that leads to maturity. Thus the parameters of development shift toward marking the progress of affiliative relationship. (Gilligan 1982, p. 170)

Belenky found similar differences in the learning patterns of women and men. She labels women's leaning styles as "connected knowing" as opposed to a traditional "male" style of "separate knowing." "Connected knowing" is more experiential learning, a way of entering into a new frame of reference by placing oneself within the new context as a way to understand it. Belenky believes this leads to women's greater experiences of empathy (Belenky et al. 1986).

Several other authors have described the world of women differently from that previously interpreted by men. Carol Stack, in her study of the Black family, found clusters and networks of exchange and care where other researchers had previously seen chaos and disorganization. She did this by redefining the "family" to include clusters of kin and nonkin that did not necessarily live together. The family comprised mostly close adult females who maintained a sophisticated web of goods and services, who could be reliably called on for help, and who sustained and protected each other (Stack 1975).

In *Worlds of Pain*, Lillian Rubin also uses the lenses of relationships and care, as well as social subordination, to examine the lives of working-class women (Rubin 1976).

Within the context of Self-In-Relation theory, a person's failure to form attachments and make affiliations is called "disconnection." In practice, a society that defines connection as either "dependence" or "smothering" and devalues relational qualities as "weaknesses" makes it difficult for women to maintain empathetic relationships and thus to value their relational capacities. This often leads women to feelings of powerlessness, anxiety, low self-esteem, and depression. Women can frequently doubt their own worth due to perceived failures in sustaining mutual relationships (Kaplan 1984).

The incongruity between their relational and connected experiences and society's definition of maturity as independence and self-sufficiency can cause women to feel disconnected from their experiences, to compromise their ability to act on their perceptions, and, as Gilligan states, to lose "their own voices" (Surrey 1987; Gilligan 1982).

Brown, in a study of depression in women in a London borough and on a Scottish island, identified the absence of a close confiding relationship as one of four vulnerability factors associated with the onset of depression in women who face adverse life experiences (Brown & Harris 1978). Belle found that a major barrier to depression for women who experience stressful life events is the presence of an intimate confidante (Belle 1982). And studies by Weissman and Klerman found that the majority of women who sought therapy for depression had experienced a relational loss within the six months preceding the onset of their depression (Weissman & Klerman 1979).

Many writers have commented on the social isolation, loneliness, depression, and low self-esteem of alcohol and other drug-dependent women. In a study of alcoholic women, Corrigan found depression to be the paramount illness of women entering treatment (Corrigan 1980). In addition, disruptive early life experiences and losses appear to be very common in the backgrounds of chemically dependent women (Gomberg 1980).

It is difficult to know if social isolation and depression is a cause, a symptom, or a consequence of chemical dependency. Addiction treatment professionals do know that alcohol and other drug-dependent women experience multiple social and personal losses and disconnections that often lead them to a deep sense of isolation.

Some of the common disconnections in the lives of alcohol- and other drug-dependent women are: the loss of parents due to separation, divorce, or death; the inaccessibility of parents due to parental preoccupation with alcohol and other drugs; a sense of loss due to inconsistent and/or neglectful parenting and poor role modeling; a sense of loss and disconnection due to a family or community climate of abuse and violence; and the loss of significant others as a child (including siblings, relatives, family, and friends) and as an adult (including spouse, children, and friends).

The pain and anxiety caused by such severe disruptions may cause a woman to turn to alcohol and other drugs for relief. Because of the centrality of relationships in a woman's life, this isolation, which is exacerbated by alcohol and other drug use, can be terrifying and destructive to her sense of self (Finkelstein & Derman 1990). Isolation can be a terrifying and destructive feeling for women, especially if they blame themselves for the exclusion and if they believe themselves to be powerless or unable to change the situation (Miller 1988).

Unfortunately, what could be labeled an "individual" treatment approach has historically been the model of care applied to chemically dependent men and women. Since most treatment programs were designed initially for and by men, little attention has been paid to the different and unique needs of women, including the larger relational context of women's lives. The traditional approach to addictions treatment is based on a medical model that views the "illness" as the individual's problem and pays scant attention in treatment to other family members or significant others, including dependent children. Relational issues have traditionally been regarded as trivial, as a distraction from the "real" issues of sobriety, and as situated outside the appropriate scope of work for recovery programs.

This approach, while never fitting well with alcohol and other drug-using women, is clearly inadequate when treating pregnant and parenting women. The lives of pregnant women and of women with children are intimately entwined with multiple individual and "systems" relationships that may include social agencies, hospitals, courts, and schools, among others. Some of these relationships are healthy, but many are destructive and dysfunctional. Without recognizing the importance of these relationships in women's lives and encompassing them *within* the treatment program, we are taking an extremely limited approach to helping women's growth and development. It is essential not to blindly push "independence" or "separation" but instead to teach women how to negotiate satisfying and supportive relationships. Treatment providers should help the chemically dependent woman to examine past relationships, including issues of loss, violence, and incest; to validate and build upon her relational skills and needs; to learn how to parent successfully; and to let go of problematic, abusive relationships.

The following sections follow a relational, life-span perspective by examining alcohol and other drug-dependent women in relationships as daughters, as partners, as parents, and, by extension, as neighbors, workers, and community members.

WOMEN IN RELATIONSHIPS

Women as Daughters

Most studies indicate that a significant percentage of addicted women were raised in families in which one or both parents were chemically dependent. Studies also indicate that children of alcoholics and other drug users are at risk for a range of social and psychological problems, including addiction, antisocial behavior, and depression. Patterns and roles developed during childhood in response to parental alcohol and drug use may cease to be healthy, effective, and growth-producing for an adult.

Variables, such as a woman's age, when her parents began to use alcohol and/or drugs, whether one or both parents were substance abusers (and which parent), the presence of violence and/or sexual abuse in her family of origin, her family of origin's economic situation, the extent of familial disruption caused by parental alcohol and other drug use, and the presence or absence of social supports can have a dramatic impact on the treatment and recovery of an addicted woman.

Although a great deal has been written about children from chemically dependent families, most of the literature comes from clinical observations, not from empirically designed studies. In addition, such studies have traditionally focused on the pathologies and weaknesses of children raised by alcohol and drug-dependent parents rather than on their strengths and adaptive capabilities. Until somewhat recently, studies of children from chemically dependent families have focused much less on daughters than on sons, reflecting the lack of gender-specific research in this area.

While most of the research is based on alcoholic families, characteristics and outcomes are frequently generalized to drug-dependent or other "dysfunctional" families. Characteristics believed to be shared by many of these families include conflict, chaos, disruption, inconsistency and unpredictability, arbitrariness, anger, violence, incest, denial, lack of trust, and financial instability.

Claudia Black has reported from clinical studies that the three major rules taught to children growing up in alcoholic families are not to talk, not to trust, and not to feel. These rules become rigid in adulthood and may cause problems in areas of trust, intimacy, control, and expression of feelings (Black 1982). In a study of 400 adult children of alcoholics, Black found that adult daughters were twice as likely to become alcoholic as those in the control group. In addition, adult children answered "yes" twice as frequently to questions about problems with trust, dependency, identifying and expressing feelings, intimacy, and depression (Cutter 1985). Woititz, among others, describes the problem adult children have in identifying what "normal" is (Woititz 1983). ✓

Dr. Susan Beletsis identified four dilemmas that she observed among adult children at the Stanford Alcohol Clinic. These were: separation from their alcoholic family (many had "unfinished business" with their family of origin which prevented them from perceiving themselves as adequate and competent); denial of needs and feelings (daughters who grew up with a disease whose critical mechanism is denial often continued to use denial as a coping mechanism); responsibility and control (many adult daughters felt responsible for their alcoholic parents' welfare and were still struggling to "control" a family situation that cannot be controlled); alcohol use and abuse (the meaning of alcohol in their own lives and the fear of becoming alcoholic were of central importance to these adult daughters of alcoholics) (Beletsis 1982).

A study conducted in 1987 of outpatient clients at a women's addictions treatment center found that the majority (more than 80 percent) of clients were children of alcoholic parents, whose lives had been significantly disrupted due to parental alcoholism. The pain, anger, and sorrow associated with parental alcoholism was still very much present in the lives of these women, even if the women had been sober for many years (Finkelstein 1987).

Treatment programs need to be cognizant of family of origin issues and recognize the impact such issues may have on a woman's own sobriety and recovery. The process of role redefinition can be complex, and making changes in lifelong patterns can be anxiety-provoking and painful. Such efforts typically require ongoing treatment and support by a skilled therapist during the recovery process.

Women as Partners

✓A significant number of chemically dependent women are involved in intimate relationships with other alcoholics and drug users. Most research suggests that women's drug and alcohol use is particularly dependent on the initiation, assistance, and encouragement of other people. According to a national study conducted by Sharon Wilsnack, the consequences women experienced due to drinking were strongly related to the drinking behavior of their husbands or partners. More specifically, Wilsnack found that women with husbands or partners who drank frequently were more likely to report drinking-related problems and symptoms of alcohol dependence than women whose husbands or partners were non-drinkers or occasional drinkers (Wilsnack 1984).

A study conducted at a women's treatment program also found that alcoholic women who had grown up in alcoholic families were significantly more likely to be involved with other alcohol and other drug users, as compared to non-alcoholic women also from chemically dependent families. In addition, the alcoholic women were more likely to have been involved in violent relationships than the non-alcoholic women (Finkelstein 1987). Women who use illicit drugs are commonly introduced to and supplied drugs by male partners. A recent study of adolescent mothers found that a partner's drug use was the most significant factor in an adolescent mother's own drug use. Adolescent mothers were at greatest risk for escalation of their own drug use if they were involved with partners who used drugs (Amaro et al. 1990).

Searching for "connection" often leads women to consume drugs and/or alcohol to "please" their partner, to have a "common activity," or simply to be able to "be in a relationship" with another person. Unfortunately, the use of drugs or alcohol leads not to greater connection but to increased "disconnection," often creating a downward spiral of searching for connection, leading to alcohol and drug use, leading to further disconnection, leading to more alcohol and drug use, and so forth. Too often a woman's substance abuse escalates to the point where she becomes dependent on her partner to supply her drugs. Therefore, alcohol and drug use, which may start in a connected relationship, often ends by destroying a woman's capacity for relationships.

All women, whether or not they use alcohol or drugs, are taught many things about relationships including to deny one's own needs; to take care of one's partner, including putting his or her needs first; to blame oneself for all of the problems in the relationship; to be totally involved with one partner to the exclusion of other significant relationships, such as friends; and to find it difficult to express anger about and/or within the relationship.

For the most part, our culture teaches us that "nice ladies" are silent, tearful, self-critical, avoid conflict, and keep anger to themselves. The "not nice lady" is unfeminine, nags, complains, voices anger ineffectively, incurs others' disapproval and "pushes people away."

For chemically dependent women, these issues may be magnified and intensified. A woman who feels extremely helpless and has low self-esteem frequently will remain in an unhealthy, abusive relationship because being alone is perhaps more terrifying. Staying in such relationships can confirm a self-perception of being worthless and unlovable. Many alcohol and other drug-dependent women have had no prior experiences with supportive or "mutual" relationships, have been accustomed to problems and pain in relationships, and often have trouble believing that they "deserve better."

At the Coalition on Addiction, Pregnancy and Parenting, we recognize the importance of validating women's strengths in relationships and helping women build on these strengths, rather than viewing all relationships as negative or "weaknesses." Counselors model "healthy," "mutual" relationships by paying close attention to issues of power and hierarchy within the counseling relationship and by being open, honest, trustworthy, and encouraging. Couples and family groups are offered counseling when appropriate. Counselors also help women learn how to trust others and to develop other non-sexual relationships and friendships. Developing a network of support is an important part of putting an intimate relationship within a new context. Counselors assist women to distinguish healthy dependency and love from unhealthy, destructive relationships. In both women's groups and individual counseling sessions, as well as "family/couple" sessions, a counselor assists a woman in learning to make decisions and choices and to express her own needs, with the recognition that developing new behaviors and attitudes towards partnership takes time.

Sexuality

Sexuality issues for chemically dependent women include guilt over sexual behavior while using drugs and alcohol, sexual preference confusion and concerns, sexual trauma histories, and sexual dysfunction. Many addicted women frequently cannot imagine, and may never have had, a sexual relationship without drugs or alcohol. ✓

Drunkenness and drug use in women is not simply associated but is equated with "rampant sexuality" and promiscuity. Common stereotypes of chemically dependent women include terms such as "tramp," "lush," "whore" (Finkelstein 1990; Finkelstein 1993; Kumpfer 1991; Mondanaro 1989; Sandmaier 1992). While early cocaine use does appear to be sexually stimulating, over time it may contribute to lessened physical sensations and disinterest. With the use of alcohol and most drugs, in fact, lack of sexual interest is more common than promiscuity. Most studies show that women who use alcohol and other drugs are more likely to be victims of the alcohol/drug-related aggression of others (Blume 1986).

In early sobriety, women may fear sexual involvements if, in the past, intimacy was predominantly connected to drinking or using other drugs. Given the high percentage of chemically dependent women with sexual trauma histories, sexuality is often associated with violence and abuse. The resulting fear, anger, and lack of trust can become major issues in sexual functioning and enjoyment. In addition, sexual relationships can trigger painful memories of past abuse that may be difficult for a woman to cope with, while attempting to abstain from alcohol and other drug use (Kovach 1986; Yandow 1989).

Research shows that chronic use of drugs and alcohol may lead to sexual dysfunction (Beckman 1979; Blume 1986; Wilsnack et al. 1991). Most women are not aware of the toxic effects of drugs and alcohol on the hormonal and nervous systems and need education in this area. Otherwise, sexual dysfunction in early sobriety may lead to self-blame and decreased self-esteem, increasing the likelihood of a return to alcohol and/or drug use. Recovering women need to understand that lack of sexual functioning in sobriety is both a physiological and psychological condition. The body may be depleted and exhausted in early sobriety by the artificial stimulation of drugs, and it often takes time for sexual desire and responsiveness to return. If sexual concerns and fears are left alone in treatment and secrets persist, they can become a major relapse concern. A woman's search for intimacy and connection will too often lead her back to self-destructive and unsatisfying sexual relationships that are frequently accompanied by alcohol and other drug use.

Family Violence

Family violence and incest are major disruptions, or "disconnections," that profoundly affect the lives of all women, particularly, it appears, those of alcohol and other drug-dependent women. Chemically dependent women are frequently victims of violence throughout their lives, including early childhood physical abuse, incest, rape, battering, and random community-wide violence (Bollerud 1990; Hurley 1989; Ludwig & Anderson 1989; Miller et al. 1993; Root 1989).

Research and clinical reports have shown a significant correlation between physical and sexual abuse and alcohol and drug use in women. Studies of women in treatment have reported that anywhere from 30 to 80 percent are victims of incest, and a study conducted at a women's outpatient treatment center in 1987 reported that 57 percent of the alcoholic women who were also adult daughters of alcoholic parents were incest survivors. The incest, which began at a mean age of eight, was usually of long-term duration. More than 50 percent of the women in this sample also reported physical violence between their parents, and 25 percent reported having been physically abused as children, primarily by alcoholic fathers who were almost always drinking at the time of the abuse (Finkelstein 1987). A study by Wilsnack reported that as many as 74 percent of alcoholic and drug-dependent women had been victims of sexual abuse (Wilsnack 1984). A study by Covington of 35 alcoholic women found that 74 percent had been sexually abused and 53 percent physically abused, with most cases of abuse having been multiple and chronic in nature. In a study of 4,729 women between the ages of 18 and 45, Miller et al. (1993) found that two thirds of the alcoholic women had experienced some form of childhood sexual abuse compared to one fifth of drinking drivers and one third of the household sample. Alcoholic women also experienced greater levels of each type of sexual abuse (for example, penetration) as compared to the drinking drivers or the random household sample (Miller et al. 1993).

√ Finally, Amaro et al. reported that 7 percent of a sample of 1,243 pregnant, predominantly poor, minority urban women reported having experienced physical or sexual violence during pregnancy. Victims were more likely to be users of drugs and alcohol and to have partners who used marijuana and cocaine. After controlling for other variables, the study found that a woman's alcohol use during pregnancy and her partner's drug use were independently associated with an increased risk of being a victim of violence during pregnancy √ (Amaro et al. 1990).

It is crucial for service providers to address issues of violence and sexual abuse at intake by asking appropriate questions in a way that validates a woman's experience and helps her to acknowledge that she is not unique or alone. It is also important to question a woman's family members about violence and abuse in a way that is nonthreatening and nonjudgmental and that lets them know that violence frequently occurs in combination with alcohol and other drug use.

In the past treatment facilities have considered violence and trauma issues to be a distraction from the primary addiction problem. This is but one example of the types of issues that are neglected when the relational concerns of a patient are not addressed or are "trivialized" in treatment. If women are not directly questioned, many cases of abuse will most likely go unreported and untreated. There is increasing clinical evidence that many chemically dependent women experience a great deal of difficulty in sobriety and frequently relapse if violence and sexual abuse issues are not addressed in treatment (Kovach 1986; Root 1989). Many women who have experienced extreme violence and sexual abuse present with symptoms that can be grouped under the diagnostic category of post-traumatic stress disorder (PTSD) (Root 1989). In addition, some research suggests that there may be an intergenerational transmission of family violence as there is a demonstrated intergenerational transmission of alcoholism. Therefore, caregivers should consider the prevention of abuse and trauma problems in future generations also to be a priority.

The timing of treatment and intervention may differ depending on a woman's sobriety and on whether the physical or sexual abuse is current or occurred many years ago. Such information should nevertheless be solicited immediately, and referrals for treatment should be made as soon as possible. For example, a woman in early sobriety may begin to experience flashbacks, similar to a post-traumatic stress reaction, of memories she had repressed, possibly through the use of drugs or alcohol. Although it is often preferable to avoid major "uncovering" work in this area during very early sobriety, this may not always be possible to avoid if relapse or "revictimization" is to be prevented. Understanding the serious long-term effects of violence, sexual abuse and incest on a woman's emotional and intellectual functioning and assisting her in developing the coping skills necessary to work through these issues as well as prevent alcohol and drug problems or relapse is critical.

Codependence

√ While recognizing the importance of paying attention to family of origin and partner relationship issues, it is perhaps not helpful in the long run for women to view themselves through such labels as "codependent" or "para-alcoholics." The concept of codependence has evolved from examining the responses of immediate family members of alcoholics, to a diagnostic category fitting anyone who has grown up in a "dysfunctional family," to labeling codependence as a "disease" and "addiction" encompassing the total society (Gomberg 1989).√

When examined from the vantage point of the relational model, the term "codependence" is problematic. Instead of building on women's relational strengths, such as empathy and nurturing, the term implies that dependence is entirely negative, and it criticizes and stigmatizes women's caretaking efforts as sick or unhealthy. Since it is primarily women who are labeled codependent, the word "dependence" is once again being used to devalue the importance of relationships in women's lives without distinguishing between unhealthy, destructive relationships and healthy interconnections (Finkelstein 1990).

In many ways, the "codependence movement" has taken the issues and concerns of contemporary women and placed them in an individual disease model rather than in a broader sociopolitical one. For example, most of the issues discussed as particular to adult children of alcoholics, including powerlessness, lack of control, loss, sensitivity to separation and abandonment, and violence, are common themes in many women's lives. Even though women are socialized to perform nurturing roles, codependence theory labels this as dysfunctional and holds women responsible for the constraints of the roles they have been reared to adopt (Epstein 1990).

Codependence also presumes that people have predetermined, rigid, responsive modes or personality characteristics, a finding not supported by research. Indeed, it was common in the 1940s through the 1960s to describe the wives of alcoholics as dysfunctional and even to blame them for their husbands' drinking problems. The historical labeling of wives of alcoholics as dependent, frustrated, sick, and pathological was a precursor to the current tendency to view all female family members of alcoholics and drug addicts as dysfunctional.

The issue is not one of simplistically categorizing women as "dependent," but a recognition that the problem faced by many addicted women is one of unequal, nonmutual relationships. With this in mind, our goal should be to support a woman's relational strengths and to help her to build mutually empowering relationships (Surrey 1987).

> Our goal as mental health professionals should be to widen rather than restrict the options available to explain and ameliorate human suffering. . . . The codependence concept has provided many people with an explanation of their experiences but the clusters of behavior currently being labeled as codependent are more than pathological entities. Additional explanations are needed that link the personal experiences of individuals with the social, ecological and political contexts in which all of us live. (Epstein & Epstein 1990, p. 7)

Women as Parents

✓ A significant number of chemically dependent women are mothers or pregnant women, many of whom also have other young children. Unfortunately, addiction prevention, intervention, and treatment programs—even those designed specifically for women—have all too frequently ignored this reality of women's lives and have paid scant attention to the myriad issues that surround alcohol and drug-dependent mothers, including: feelings of guilt and shame; the difficulties of being a single parent; the care and responsibility of children during the women's early stages of sobriety; the lack of access to treatment facilities; anger and blame from caregivers; the need for parenting skills training and knowledge of infant care and child development; the potential for child abuse and neglect; and the lack of medical and other supportive services, such as prenatal care, housing, and child care.

From a relational perspective, the birth of a new infant offers a mother the opportunity for a new, caring relationship. However, this period can also be one of increased fear and anxiety regarding the health of her newborn as well as extreme guilt regarding issues of addiction and parenting. The guilt that many chemically dependent mothers already feel is reinforced and exacerbated by the significant societal stigma that surrounds addicted mothers. Treatment providers are not immune to this stigma and may also respond with anger toward the addicted mother. We all identify with the helpless child since, after all, we were all once children. Persons raised within families affected by substance abuse may have unresolved issues from their own childhood that are frequently projected onto the addicted mother. It is critical that staff examine their own attitudes and personal history (including being raised in chemically dependent families) if they are to assist alcohol and drug-dependent mothers confront the guilt, stigma, and shame they feel as they begin the recovery process.

The Empowerment Approach

The relational model helps us to frame an empowerment approach for addicted women by focusing on strengths rather than deficits. For example, many pregnant addicted women view their current pregnancy as a "new beginning," a chance to "do it right this time." A woman should be supported and encouraged to build on these feelings and to focus on her ability to nurture and care for others. Treatment providers should give women messages of empowerment such as "I believe you can do this" and assist them in learning how to deal with crucial life issues such as health care, employment, infant care and development, child care, housing, and parenting.

Mothers of young children are frequently overwhelmed with the tasks ahead of them; it is difficult, with limited financial and emotional resources, to stay sober and drug-free while raising children. To expect a woman alcoholic or drug addict to be able to manage recovery without receiving additional services and support for her parenting role is both unrealistic and unfair. An empowerment approach is essential if we are to assist mothers in modifying how they perceive themselves. Doing too much for a mother may reinforce for her that she is incapable of doing things for herself, while not doing enough could reinforce her perceptions of herself as incompetent and a failure (Egeland & Erickson 1990).

Recovery

While it is extremely important for service providers to convey hope for the future, it is also important for them to assist chemically dependent women to have realistic expectations for themselves and for their children. This includes helping a woman to learn the range of what is "normal" in infant and child development so she does not blame herself or expect to have the "perfect" baby. It is common for a woman newly in recovery to have unrealistically high expectations of herself. This is easily transferred to a new baby, especially when so much of a woman's identity and self-esteem is involved.

The "disease" model of addictions is useful in helping a woman understand that she and her family have suffered from the consequences of alcoholism and drug abuse, not her intentional or deliberate behavior, and that her options were limited during her period of active drinking and drug use (Finkelstein 1981; Finkelstein, Duncan et al. 1990; Finkelstein 1994). It is critical that caregivers offer messages of hope and the possibility of change as well as assist a woman in finding the tools and supports she needs to stay drug free and parent effectively without being overwhelmed with the multiple tasks involved (Finkelstein 1994; Finkelstein & Derman 1991; Weiner & Larsson 1987; Weiner, Rosett & Mason, 1985).

Recovery programs should expect that a pregnant woman's focus will be split between her own recovery and her anxieties, fears, and concerns regarding pregnancy, delivery, and the impact of a new baby on her life. This can be frustrating for caregivers, who may perceive a woman's preoccupation with her pregnancy and new-born as an "avoidance" of recovery issues. It is natural, however, for a woman to focus inward during her pregnancy and is not necessarily a sign of her lack of commitment to recovery. For this reason, the recovery process can take longer for pregnant women and new mothers. It is crucial for caregivers to expect and under-stand this dynamic and to offer the woman support for the conflicts she is feeling and will continue to feel about recovery and parent-ing. The best way to assist a woman in this area is to conceptualize a model of treatment (such as the relational model) that is able to integrate all perspectives and life issues into a holistic recovery plan for a woman and her children.

Parenting

Much of the psychological literature makes it clear that in order to nurture others, a person must first be nurtured herself. As de-scribed previously, chemically dependent women frequently come from disruptive and chaotic childhoods in which they received little or no nurturing. Certainly, since so many are adult children of alcoholic and drug-dependent parents, they may never have been exposed to healthy and/or appropriate parenting role models.

At some point in their recovery, addicted mothers need to come to terms with their own past behaviors—particularly with regard to their own children—and begin to see a connection between their childhood and how they are raising or wish to raise their own children. Studies of adult representations of early attachment expe-riences indicate a significant link between how a mother views her own history and the quality of her attachment to her baby.

The important variable appears to be how a mother perceives the quality of care she received in the past, not the actual quality of care she may or may not have received (Main & Goldwyn 1984; Egeland & Erickson 1990). Since so many of the alcohol and drug-dependent women seen in treatment were physically or sexually abused as children, this work is even more important if the intergenerational transmission of both violence and addiction is to be prevented.

Parenting is obviously a *relational* process—one that deeply af-fects and changes both mother and child. But as Janet Surrey sug-gests, Winnicott's (1965) "good enough mother," who is capable of providing the child with an empathetic environment, does not appear suddenly upon the birth of an infant (Surrey 1985). A chemically dependent mother must have assistance in learning both how to parent and how to be empathetic in reestablishing relationships with her child/children. Her child/children will also need help and support during this period to deal with the consequences for them of their mother's alcohol and drug use, to understand treatment and recovery, and to reestablish a relationship with their mother. Children should not be treated as "appendages" to a mother in treatment but have needs of their own which are crucial to address (Pearlman et al. 1980).

A woman who is overwhelmed with the tasks of parenting, as well as inadequate housing, a lack of financial, health care, and child-care resources, and who has few family or social support systems in place is extremely vulnerable to relapse. Service professionals must begin to develop comprehensive, coordinated, "relational" models of care for a mother and her children in which addictions prevention and treatment are integrated with the full range of other required services.

CONCLUSION

As the United States continues to experience the significant impact of alcohol and other drug use on women and children, it is important that chemical dependency professionals begin to reformulate prevention and treatment efforts within a more comprehensive, coordinated, family-centered or "relational" approach. This article has presented a theoretical model, adapted from the self-in-relation model, which can help guide professionals as they seek new approaches and frameworks for the delivery of services to chemically dependent women. This framework will aid in understanding women's lives from both a multi-generational and lifespan perspective. Successful prevention and treatment efforts require us to examine, and perhaps restructure, the health, education, and social services systems currently available to America's women, children, and their families.

REFERENCES

Amaro, H., Freed, L., Cabral, H., & Zuckerman, B. (1990). Violence during pregnancy and substance use. *American Journal of Public Health. 80*(5), 575-579.

Beckman, L. (1979). Reported effects of alcohol on the sexual feelings and behavior of women alcoholics and non-alcoholics. *Journal of Studies on Alcohol, 40*, 272-282.

Belenky, M., Clincky, B., Goldberger, N., & Tarule, J. (1986). *Woman's way of knowing: The development of self, voice and mind.* New York: Basic Books, Inc.

Beletsis, S. (1982). *From generation to generation: The adult children of alcoholics.* Unpublished document, Stanford Alcohol Clinic.

Belle, D. (Ed.) (1982). *Lives in stress: Women and depression.* Beverly Hills, CA: Sage Publications.

Black, C. (1982). *It will never happen to me.* Denver, CO: Mac Printing and Publications Division.

Blume, S. (1986, September 19). Women and alcohol: A review. *Journal of the American Medical Association, 256*(11), 1467-1470.

Bolleuid, K. (1990). A model for the treatment of trauma-related syndromes among chemically dependent inpatient women. *Journal of Substance Abuse Treatment, 7*, 83-87.

Brown, G.W., & Harris, T. (1978). *Social origins of depression: A study of psychiatric disorders in women.* New York: The Free Press.

Corrigan, E. (1980). *Alcoholic women in treatment.* New York: Oxford University Press.

Covington, S. (1982). *Sex and violence–the unmentionables in alcoholism treatment.* Paper presented at the National Alcoholism Forum, Washington, DC.

Cutter, C. (1985). *How do people change in Alanon? Reports of adult children of alcoholics.* Doctoral dissertation, Heller School, Brandeis University.

Egeland, B., & Erickson, M. (1990). Rising above the past: Strategies for helping new mothers break the cycle of abuse and neglect. *Zero to Three* (Bulletin, Center for Clinical Infant Programs), *11*(2).

Epstein, M., & Epstein, K. (1990, September). Codependence as social narrative. *Readings: A Journal of Reviews and Commentary in Mental Health.*

Finkelstein, N. (1994, February). Treatment issues for alcohol and drug-dependent pregnant and parenting women. *Health & Social Work, 19*(1), 7-15.

Finkelstein, N. (1993). Treatment programming for alcohol and drug dependent pregnant women. *The International Journal of the Addictions, 28*(13), 1275-1309.

Finkelstein, N. (1987). *Effects of parental alcoholism, family violence and social support on the inter-generational transmission of alcoholism in adult women.* Doctoral dissertation, Heller School, Brandeis University.

Finkelstein, N., & Derman, L. (1990). Women as single parents: What can a mother do? *Reaching women about alcohol and other drugs.* New York: Scarecrow Press.

Finkelstein, N., Duncan, S., Derman, L., & Smeltz, J. (1990). *Getting sober, getting well: A treatment guide for caregivers who work with women.* Cambridge, MA: Women's Alcoholism Program/CASPAR, Inc.

Gilligan, C. (1982). *In a different voice.* Cambridge, MA: University Press.

Gomberg, E. (1989). *On terms used and abused: The concept of "co-dependency."* Unpublished paper.

Gomberg, E. (1980). Risk factors related to alcohol problems among women: Proneness and vulnerability. *Alcohol and women: Research monograph no. one,* National Institute on Drug Abuse (DHHS Publication No. ADM 80-8-35). Washington, DC: Supt. of Docs., U.S. Government Printing Office.

Hurley, D. (1991). Women, alcohol and incest: An analytical review. *Journal of Studies on Alcohol, 5*(3), 253-268.

Jordan, J., Surrey, J., & Kaplan, H. (1983). *Women and empathy: Implications for psychological development and psychotherapy.* (Work in Progress), Stone Center, Wellesley College, No. 02.

Kaplan, A. (1984). *The "self-in-relation": Implications for depression in women.* (Work in Progress), Stone Center, Wellesley College, No. 14.

Kovach, J. (1986). Incest as a treatment issue for alcoholic women. *Alcoholism Treatment Quarterly, 3*(1), 1-15.

Kumpfer, K.L. (1991). Treatment programs for drug abusing women. *Future Child, 1*(1), 50-59.

Ludwig, G.B., & Andersen, M.D. (1989). Substance abuse in women: Relationship between chemical dependency of women and past reports of physical and/or sexual abuse. *The International Journal of the Addictions, 24*(8).

Main, M., & Goldwyn, R. (1984). Predicting rejection of her infant from mother's representation of her own experiences: Implications for the abused-abusing intergenerational cycle. *Child Abuse and Neglect, 8,* 203-217.

Miller, J.B. (1988). *Connections, disconnections and violations.* (Work in Progress), Stone Center, Wellesley College, No. 33.

Miller, J.B. (1986). *What do we mean by relationships?* (Work in Progress), Stone Center, Wellesley College, No. 22.

Miller, J.B. (1984). *Development of women's sense of self.* (Work in Progress), Stone Center, Wellesley College, No. 12.

Miller, B.A., Downs, U.R., & Testa, M. (1993). Interrelationships between victimization experiences and women's alcohol use. *Journal of Studies on Alcohol,* Supplement *11,* 109-117.

Mondanaro, J. (1989). *Chemically dependent women: Assessment and treatment.* Boston, MA: Lexington Books.

Pearlman, P., West, M., & Dalton, J. *Mothers and children together: Parenting in a substance abuse program.* Unpublished document. Philadelphia, PA: Family House.

Root, M.D. (1989, October). Treatment failures: The role of sexual victimization in women's addictive behavior. *American Journal of Orthopsychiatry, 59*(4).

Rubin, L. (1976). *Worlds of pain.* New York: Basic Books.

Sandmaier, M. (1992). *The invisible alcoholics: Women and alcohol* (2nd ed.). New York: McGraw Hill.

Stack, C. (1975). *All our kin: strategies for survival in a black community.* New York: Harper and Row.

Surrey, J. (1987). *Relationships and empowerment.* (Work in Progress), Stone Center, Wellesley College, No. 30.

Surrey, J. (1985). *Self-in-relation: a theory of women's development.* (Work in Progress), Stone Center, Wellesley College, No. 13.

Weiner, L., & Larsson, G. (1987). Clinical prevention of fetal alcohol effects–a reality: Evidence for the effectiveness of intervention. *Alcohol Health & Research World, 12*(4), 60-66.

Weiner, L., Rosett, H.L., & Mason, E.A. (1985). Training professionals to identify and treat pregnant women who drink heavily. *Alcohol, Health & Research World, 10*(11), 32-37.

Weissman, M.M., & Klerman, G.L. (1979). Sex differences and the etiology of depression. In: E.S. Gombey, & V. Franks (Eds.), *Gender and disordered behavior.* New York: Brunner/Mazel.

Wilsnack, S. (1984). Drinking, sexuality and sexual dysfunctions in women. In: S. Wilsnack, & L. Beckman (Eds.), *Alcohol problems in women.* New York: Guilford Press.

Wilsnack, S., Klassen, A., Scheer, B., & Wilsnack, R. (1991, March). Predicting onset and chronicity of women's problem drinking: A five year longitudinal analysis. *American Journal of Public Health, 81*(3), 305-314.

Winnicott, D.W. (1965). *The maturational process and the facilitating environment.* London: Hogarth Press.

Woititz, J. (1983). *Adult children of alcoholics.* FL: Health Communications.

Yandow, V. (1989, May). Alcoholism in women. *Psychiatric Annals, 19*(5), 243-247.

Retaining Your Clients and Your Sanity:
Using a Relational Model
of Multi-Systems Case Management

Laurie S. Markoff, PhD
Patricia A. Cawley, MSW, LICSW, BCD

SUMMARY. Addressing women's special needs in substance abuse treatment might increase the retention of women clients. This paper reviews the theoretical and empirical support for the use of two particular strategies, an emphasis on relationship and an empowerment approach. One particular program, Project Second Beginning, which utilizes a relational model of multi-systems case management to address women's special needs, is described in detail. This program has had an unusually high retention rate. Case illustrations are used to illustrate the implementation of the model. *[Article copies available from The Haworth Document Delivery Service: 1-800-342-9678. E-mail address: getinfo@haworth.com]*

Research on substance abuse treatment has repeatedly shown that the longer the client remains in treatment, the better the outcome

---

Laurie S. Markoff is Executive Director of Associates for Human Potential, Inc., 323 Boston Post Road, Sudbury, MA 01776. Patricia A. Cawley is also affliated with the Associates for Human Potential, Inc.

This publication was made possible by grant number SPO2383 from the Center for Substance Abuse Prevention. These contents are solely the responsibility of the authors and do not necessarily represent the official views of the Center for Substance Abuse Prevention.

[Haworth co-indexing entry note]: "Retaining Your Clients and Your Sanity: Using a Relational Model of Multi-Systems Case Management." Markoff, Laurie S. and Patricia A. Cawley. Co-published simultaneously in *Journal of Chemical Dependency Treatment* (The Haworth Press, Inc.) Vol. 6, No. 1/2, 1996, pp. 45-65; and: *Chemical Dependency: Women at Risk* (ed: Brenda L. Underhill, and Dana G. Finnegan) The Haworth Press, Inc., 1996, pp. 45-65; and: *Chemical Dependency: Women at Risk* (ed: Brenda L. Underhill, and Dana G. Finnegan) Harrington Park Press, an imprint of The Haworth Press, Inc., 1996, pp. 45-65. Single or multiple copies of this article are available from The Haworth Document Delivery Service [1-800-342-9678, 9:00 a.m. - 5:00 p.m. (EST) E-mail address: getinfo@haworth.com].

45

(Aron & Daily, 1977; Simpson, 1979). Therefore, the fact that drop-out rates from all modalities of substance abuse treatment are relatively high is of serious concern (Allison & Hubbard, 1985). The few studies which attempt to compare drop-out rates for men and women have reported complex interactions between gender and other variables, rather than differences in overall retention rates (Stark, 1992). There appear to be differences in the factors that determine drop-out rates for men and women, which suggests that interventions which target women's special needs might increase the retention of women clients. Project Second Beginning (PSB) is a substance abuse treatment program which was designed specifically to address the needs of women clients. Taking its theoretical basis from recent literature on women's psychotherapy, PSB attempts to address women's special needs by using a relational model of multi-systems case management. So far, this has resulted in an unusually high rate of client retention.

The present paper will review the empirical literature which suggests factors which may impact the retention of women clients. The theoretical and empirical support for the use of two particular strategies, an emphasis on relationship and an empowerment approach, will be presented. Papers which describe the outcomes of the few substance abuse treatment programs which have attempted to address women's special needs will be discussed. And finally, one particular program, PSB, will be described in detail, using clinical examples to more clearly delineate the implementation of a women-specific model of treatment.

RETENTION OF WOMEN
IN SUBSTANCE ABUSE TREATMENT

In a review of the literature published in 1975, Baekeland and Lundwall reported that women drop out of substance abuse treatment more often than men do. Since then, however, a number of studies have been published that find no difference in retention rates for male and female clients (Beck, Shemin, Fraps, Borgmeyer & Whitt, 1983; Stark & Campbell, 1988; and Steer, 1983). In a recent review of the retention literature, Stark (1992) concluded that there is a "complex relation between gender, social and personality factors, treatment modality, and dropping out." This is based on the fact that several investigations have found that gender interacts with other variables that affect retention. Greene and Ryser (1987) reported that retention of women clients is related to modality, that is, women actually drop out of detoxification, hospital, drug-free outpatient and day treatment programs less frequently than men do, although drop-out rates were high for both genders in all modalities. Sansone (1980) reported that women were more likely to leave a therapeutic community than were their male counterparts. She speculated that this was due to the fact that the treatment program had a predominantly male orientation with little provision made for meeting the special needs of women. Beckman and Bardsley (1986) found that different variables affected retention rates for women and for men. The treatment variables that affected drop-out rates for men were characteristics of the men themselves, such as more depression, lower self-efficacy and substance abuse history, or characteristics of their individual environments such as available social support and prior social stability. However, for the women, drop-out rates were affected by variables that were more specifically related to treatment. Women who believed that their behavior determined their health were more likely to remain in treatment, and programs that provided more health services were more likely to keep women clients. These authors also hypothesized that treatment variables are more important for women because treatment approaches were originally developed to work with men, and may not adequately meet the needs of women clients. This implies that programs designed to meet women's needs might be more successful at retaining women clients.

ADDRESSING WOMEN'S SPECIAL NEEDS IN SUBSTANCE ABUSE TREATMENT

Emphasis on Relationship

Improving the effectiveness of substance abuse treatment programs for women may be accomplished by paying particular attention to recent thinking about the conditions which foster emotional growth for women. Until recently, theories of psychological development generally derived from research on the development of men, and postulated that development proceeds from a state of fusion of self with object and dependency to a state of separation, individuation, and autonomy. More recent research and theory in the area of women's development (Chodorow, 1978; Gilligan, 1982; Miller, 1991) has suggested that development for women proceeds quite differently. Some current theorists describe women's development as a function of increasing capacity for depth, diversity, and articulation of the range of relationships in which women can engage (Surrey, 1991) and suggest that the best context for stimulating this emotional growth is that of one or more empathic, mutual relationships. It is through the vehicle of relationships that women's growth occurs (Kaplan, 1984). One of the mechanisms by which women grow in this relational context is through the development of empathy with past selves. That is, when other people exhibit empathy toward a woman for the circumstances and emotional stresses she experienced in the past which resulted in behaviors she herself finds unacceptable, the woman may gradually develop compassion and acceptance for the person she was in the past. This results in a reduction of shame and guilt and an increase in self-esteem which then allows the woman to devote her energy to improving her life in the present.

This "relational" model of women's development implies that a treatment program for women who abuse substances should focus on helping women to develop mutual, empathic relationships with the staff, with each other, and with the people in their lives. While many of these concepts are shared by a number of different schools of psychotherapy, the priority this model gives to focusing on the relational context is somewhat different. The model suggests that a woman's self-esteem is largely based on her view of herself within relationships, and that only by improving her functioning within relationships can her self-esteem be enhanced.

This viewpoint differs from that of traditional substance abuse treatment, which often recommends isolating the individual from her relational context so that she can focus on sobriety (Allison & Hubbard, 1985). Clients in traditional substance abuse treatment are often told they should be "selfish" about their recovery. The relational model would suggest that such statements may invite resistance in women because their sense of self is based largely on who they are in connection with others. The interests of the self and those of the other are seen as not necessarily different. Women are motivated to become drug and alcohol free in order to enhance their relationships. According to this perspective, it would be more effective to point out to women that sobriety will not only benefit them, but others in their lives as well.

In his 1977 investigation, Mulford found that women are more than twice as likely as men to cite problems in their relationships with their children as an impetus for seeking treatment. Women also responded to confrontation from important people in their lives by seeking treatment much more quickly than did men. Since a woman's self-esteem is often based on her capacity to nurture relationships and women are motivated to enter treatment by the desire to change something in the interpersonal sphere (Sandmaier, 1980), that is, by the desire to become better mothers, partners, and daughters, this desire to preserve relationships could be acknowledged as a strength and built on, rather than interpreted as resistance, as is often the case in traditional substance abuse treatment. This suggests that interventions which target the important relationships in women's lives could be included in substance abuse treatment programs as a means of increasing the retention of female clients. Substance abuse treatment could include child care arrangements, parenting education, and help for clients' troubled children (Wilson, 1991). Family therapy with families of origin could be offered for those whose families can participate. Since women often are introduced to substance abuse by men and continue to use in order to preserve those relationships (Nichols, 1985), couples counseling could be included when appropriate.

Substance-abusing women are usually separated, divorced, or partnered with substance abusing men (Beckman & Amaro, 1984). If they are not in a relationship with a substance abuser, they tend to drink and drug alone. They are often interpersonally isolated and lack social support. This suggests that focusing on the development of strong, mutual relationships with other recovering women during treatment would improve retention, enhance recovery, and help prevent relapse (Schilit & Gomberg, 1987).

Empowerment as a Therapeutic Approach

Society attaches greater blame and stigmatization to the female addict. Not surprisingly, women addicts have internalized these values and stereotypes. As a result, women who are addicted suffer from lower self-esteem than their male counterparts (Beckman, 1978). Thirty to 75 percent of women substance abusers have been victims of sexual abuse (Root, 1989), which also has an impact on self-esteem. Female substance abusers are more self-critical than men who abuse substances (Mulford, 1977) and are more likely to suffer from Primary Affective Disorder (Schuckit, 1983). These findings taken together suggest that a confrontational model of treatment is contraindicated. When people are depressed and/or have low self-esteem, confrontation tends to increase their depression and their hopelessness, which can result in their dropping out of treatment or, in the case of those who abuse substances, to relapse. In fact, the appropriate therapeutic approach with this population is one of empowerment, support, building on strengths, and helping them *not* to take responsibility for things outside of their control (Brill, 1981). It is especially important to include women in their own treatment-planning, to give them the message that they are the best experts on themselves and what they need. This can be the first step in the process of teaching them to attend to and express their own needs. It is also important to expose women to successful female role models in the form of female staff and administrators (Beckman & Amaro, 1984).

Women who abuse substances often see themselves as both worthless and powerless. It would seem appropriate to help them explore the events that led them to feel that way. This exploration would include helping them examine the messages they have gotten from society and from family about what it means to be a woman and how these messages have affected the way they feel about themselves (Underhill, 1986). Since women substance abusers often suffer from eating disorders as well (Beckman & Amaro, 1984), helping them explore their body image would be important. Discussion of sexuality and sexual identity, including education about the effects of physical and sexual abuse and the course of recovery from these trauma, is also indicated (Reed, 1985).

Although it is of therapeutic value to validate women's beliefs that being nurturing and caring for others is worthwhile, it is also of value to teach them to take care of themselves: emotionally, physically and economically. Education in the area of women's health issues and access to medical care, including a focus on the addictive properties of prescribed medications, is especially relevant to women clients. The inclusion of skill-building in the areas of assertiveness and the positive use of anger as components of substance abuse treatment (Underhill, 1986) are indicated by the finding that women's substance abuse patterns tend to emulate the patterns of those with whom they have closest contact (Harrison, 1989). Educational and vocational assessment and planning could be offered as part of treatment so that women who lack the knowledge and skills necessary to achieve economic self-sufficiency can acquire them (Reed, 1985).

ENHANCING RETENTION OF WOMEN IN SUBSTANCE ABUSE TREATMENT

If these recommendations for the treatment of women are incorporated into treatment programs, we believe that these programs will attract more women, women will stay longer, and women will have more successful treatment outcomes. Indirect support for this hypothesis is derived from a study conducted in Sweden by Dahlgren and Willander (1989). Although their study included only women who abuse alcohol, they designed a woman-specific treatment program which consisted of detoxification followed by outpatient treatment over the course of a year, and randomly assigned women to either this program or the standard coeducational alcohol treatment program. The process of treatment for the woman-specific program was characterized by individual treatment planning, involvement of significant others (including children) in the treatment, focus on women's issues, and exchange of experiences with other women. There was more improvement in social adjustment and decrease in alcohol consumption for women in the specialized program than women in the control condition. This study suggests that treatment programs which focus on meeting women's special needs can improve the outcomes of female clients.

Another example of a program enhancing retention of female clients by attending to women's special needs is reported by Stevens, Arbiter and Glider (1989). They describe an attempt by a coeducational residential treatment program to improve effectiveness with women residents. The authors instituted some of the changes recommended above, including hiring a female program director and more female staff; adding some women-only group sessions; incorporating exploration of sexuality and victimization as part of the treatment plan for all residents; placing emphasis on equality and mutuality in all relationships; providing seminars about assertiveness, women's health issues, and vocational planning; and enabling women to bring their children with them into treatment. In response to these changes, length of stay for women residents increased dramatically. Success of treatment, measured by the number of residents who remained drug-free, also increased significantly.

Project Second Beginning (PSB), which is described below, is an example of a substance abuse treatment program which was designed specifically to meet the special needs of women clients. The program uses the relational model as its theoretical base and attempts to empower women to create their own recovery. Its approach also includes access to interventions which may be used to impact the major relationships in a woman's life. This program has had unusual success in retaining women clients. Thirteen months after the program opened there were 52 clients who had completed the intake procedure six months ago or longer. Of these, 12 (23.1%) dropped out, 4 (7.7%) either terminated or moved, and 36 (69.2%) were still receiving services.

PROJECT SECOND BEGINNING

In October of 1991, Associates for Human Potential received a five-year grant from the Office of Substance Abuse Prevention, now the Center for Substance Abuse Prevention, to provide case management services to pregnant and parenting substance abusing women in what is considered the metro west/metro south area of Massachusetts. A case management model was chosen because it was believed to be the best vehicle for addressing the multiple service needs of women clients. That is, we thought that women would be more likely to remain in treatment if issues such as financial difficulties, inadequate housing, the needs of significant others and children, and other problems of importance to them could be addressed in conjunction with their substance abuse difficulties. It was felt that a *clinical* case management model would be most effective, one in which the vehicle of a therapeutic relationship would be used to help women identify their needs and utilize all the services available which would facilitate their recovery. Professional staff (social workers and psychologists with masters level training or more) were hired as case managers, because it was believed that clinicians would be most successful at developing working relationships with the women.

The service region is comprised of 45 cities and towns with a population base of over 800,000. The area is diversified geographically and by income level. Most residents of the area are Caucasian, although a small percentage are African American and Hispanic. The region includes urban, rural, and suburban communities that range from the wealthier towns to poverty stricken areas in Massachusetts.

Tables 1 and 2 illustrate the characteristics of the initial 93 first-time entrants of PSB. Most of the clients are white, most are between the ages of 21 and 35 with a good number in their late teens. Most of the women have had some high school education, but only a small number have gone beyond high school. Most are poor, and 50% of the women are single heads of households.

Table 3 illustrates the percentage of clients who reported frequent use of various classes of drugs. Alcohol is the most frequently used substance, with cocaine and marijuana coming next, followed by opiates and prescription drugs.

The project staff developed a multi-systems model of case management, as illustrated in Figure 1. Three client systems were identified: social service agencies, the women and their families, and social policy makers.

Interventions with social service agencies generally include mutual referral and provision of ongoing consultation and training. PSB attempts to maintain relationships with staff members of other agencies in order to access better services for clients. An attempt is

TABLE 1. Characteristics of First Time Entrants to Project Second Beginning (N = 99)

Race

Caucasian		74.2%
African American		15.0%
Hispanic		7.5%
Other		3.3%

Age in years

under 15		1.7%
15-17		18.3%
18-20		4.2%
21-35		53.3%
over 35		2.5%
Unknown		20.0%

TABLE 2. Educational Level and Income of First Time Entrants of Project Second Beginning (N = 99)

Years Completed in School

Elementary	5-7		2.5%
	8		2.5%
High School	1-3		47.5%
	4		24.2%
College or	1-3		15.8%
Technical	4		2.5%
Unknown			5.0%

Income

Below Federal Poverty level	54.2%
100-200% of Poverty level	15.5%
Above 200% of Poverty level	8.3%

made to address barriers frequently encountered when women who abuse substances attempt to utilize these services. Relationships with other service providers create the opportunity to correct misinformation and reshape negative bias through education, advocacy, and reframing. Collaborative processes have been established with young parents programs, substance abuse treatment programs, maternal and child health agencies, the local women's prison, area offices of child protective services, the Department of Public Wel-

TABLE 3. Self-Report of Drugs Frequently Used by First Time Entrants to Project Second Beginning (N = 99)

Alcohol	73.3%
Cocaine	50.0%
Marijuana	46.7%
Opiates	15.0%
Prescription Drugs	13.3%
Hallucinogens	12.5%
Amphetamines	5.0%
None	1.7%
Barbiturates	1.6%
Inhalants	0.8%

fare, the Department of Employment and Training, Head Start, Early Intervention, W.I.C., the Visiting Nurses Association, and various educational institutions.

The services provided to the second client system, the woman and her family, begin when a referral is made. Each woman is assigned a case manager who meets with her to do a comprehensive intake interview which covers all aspects of the woman's life: medical, economic, educational/vocational, substance abuse and recovery history, and most importantly, information about all of her significant relationships, past and present. The case manager then helps the woman to identify the areas of her life which she wishes to change. Goals are set for each area and then prioritized in terms of urgency. The case manager then identifies services which will help the woman to achieve the most urgent goals and assists the woman in accessing these services. If no readily available provider exists, PSB staff may provide services directly, for example, by offering counseling to a woman with no insurance or creating a parenting group in a region that does not have any. Once the service plan is developed, the case manager continues to meet with the client on a regular basis, to monitor her progress in utilizing services and to address any barriers, both internal and external, that the woman encounters in following through on the plan. As urgent and basic goals are achieved (such as safe housing, economic stability, early abstinence) the case manager will help the woman to identify other, more long-term goals (such as higher education, dealing with trauma history in therapy). The case

FIGURE 1. Multi-Systems Case Management Model

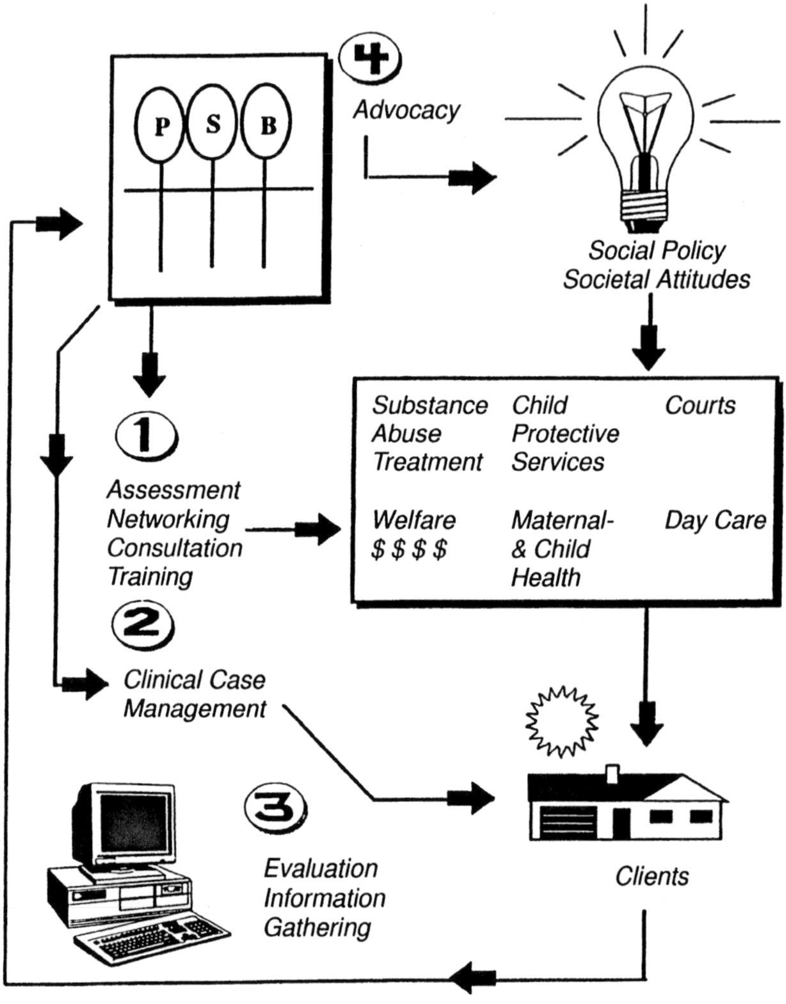

manager continues to meet with the woman regularly, but less frequently, as her service needs lessen. The relationship terminates when the woman and the case manager agree that the woman is able to pursue any remaining goals without assistance.

The mode of treatment of PSB is helping clients to obtain needed services, but its underlying philosophy is that of the "relational" model of women's development. As stated earlier, the relational theorists emphasize the importance of relationships to women's psychological growth and development. Women are seen as developing their identities within their relationships and growing through these connections with others. The relationship between the client and case manager is seen as the vehicle which holds the client through the ups and downs of recovery, guiding her through the continuum of care and the social service system. At the same time, the client is encouraged to reevaluate and improve the relationships she has in her life, in order to develop a network of mutual, empathic, supportive relationships. This usually includes referral to traditional self-help which is believed to be an integral component of a woman's recovery. However, the staff also help women sort out what is relevant for them and why.

Case Illustrations

Sharing in Group

The following are a few illustrations of ways in which the "women-specific" nature of PSB influences the process of substance abuse treatment. The first example is an excerpt from a "Women's Recovery Group." The belief that women's growth is fostered in relationships to others further supports the traditional importance of groups in substance abuse treatment. This has resulted in PSB staff facilitating a variety of different groups. It is very empowering for recovering women to share their experiences in a safe place. Members of PSB groups often contact each other outside the sessions for support. This "relating" outside of the groups is encouraged by the facilitators, in contrast to many traditional psychotherapists who prohibit contact except during sessions (Yalom, 1985). The following dialogue is from a group that had been meeting for a year. The group was processing one member's decision to terminate from the group because the evening the group met conflicted with a choir she had joined. Group members had varying responses including anger, betrayal, sadness and fear. All the members agreed that they were concerned about the exiting member's priorities. In discussing the dropping out of a particular group member (an unusual event) the other members began to explore what keeps them in treatment.

A: "I just can't understand why anybody would want to leave this group. This is the highlight of my week. I look forward to it. Really."

B: (who had earlier in the session experienced and shared intense feelings of sadness regarding an ongoing problem.) "I know. I mean, it's Monday night, this is what I do. I come here every Monday night. You know, I was fine all week, I really was. Just being here brings up all this stuff. This is the place where I deal with what's really going on."

A: (to B) "Do you tell Harry when you need him? What you need from him? I never did. I didn't think Robert could be there for me. I didn't think anybody could. I've finally learned to ask." (Delightedly) "And he does it. He's really there for me. It's amazing."

B: "Yeah, Harry is there, but, well, this is something I really need to resolve myself."

A: "Yes, but I bet if you told Harry what you are going through he'd be more helpful."

C: "I think it's much easier for men to ask for what they really need. Women are used to taking care of other people. I do it automatically. I remember when I was drinking, I would get on the phone"; (other group members are laughing as this phenomenon has been talked about before. All the members became very sociable when under the influence). "It was, I don't know. I was looking for a connection, somebody to relate to. Of course, I always thought I was fine, the person I had been talking to always knew that I had been drinking."

D: (who has social anxiety) "I know what you mean. I was so at ease with people when I was drinking." (Smiling) "I had fun. I was relaxed. I really enjoyed myself when I was drinking."

B: "Yeah, I miss that . . . "

F: "Camaraderie."

B: "Yes, there really was that sense of connecting. Even if you knew that the other person was as wasted as you were."

C: "In some ways it was superficial." (Laughing) "But I really miss it." (Serious again) "I wonder if that was what we were looking for in our drinking? That connection that we did not know how to make."

(Group is nodding in agreement.)

D: "Yeah, now the question is, how do we do it sober?"

(Pause.)

A: "I just get so much out of this group."

Utilizing the group process, the women have discovered that their drug and alcohol abuse facilitated connections with other people. By being authentic with one another in the group the members *are* learning how to make connections in sobriety. In order to make these connections, each member has had to increase her ability to identify her own needs and "ask for help." The members have increasingly taken these risks in relationships both within and outside the group. Although initially anxiety provoking, these risks have served to increase their sense of being truly connected to others. It is this sense of connection which holds them in treatment and replaces one of the needs previously met by abusing substances.

Intervention in Program

Another example of being able to meet a client's needs by being tuned into "women's specific issues" occurred with a client who had entered a residential treatment program following her relapse. The program was formerly an all male program but was now taking female clients. The case manager went to the treatment program to visit the client, S. While waiting to see S, the case manager became painfully aware of the sexualized atmosphere in the program. Clients and counselors alike freely leered at the case manager.

When the case manager met with S, she presented as extremely agitated and desperately wanted to leave the program. The case manager learned that S's relapse had been triggered by previously repressed memories of incest. Since her admission to this treatment program, she was being flooded with painful physical and psychological flashbacks. Her male counselor felt unable to help her with these feelings and was attempting to have her "prioritize" her sobriety as her number one concern.

The case manager's internal experience upon entering the program enabled her to both quickly diagnose the problem and empathically connect with the client. The case manager then intervened at multiple levels. She used her relationship with the clinical staff of the program to educate them about the needs of this particular woman in treatment. She later met with the administrative staff of the program to make suggestions regarding policy changes and training for staff that would make the program more responsive to the needs of women clients. Perhaps the most important intervention for this client, however, was "being there" for her. S was able to use her relationship with her case manager to create a "holding environment" in order to address and begin to work through the pain she was experiencing. In the context of their relationship, the case manager was able to help S to understand that she was not "going crazy," but was having flashbacks that are often part of the recovery process for women who have been sexually abused. The case manager validated S's experience by suggesting that the sexualized atmosphere of the program might be exacerbating the flashbacks. Had the case manager not intervened, S most probably would have left the treatment program in order to self-medicate her feelings.

Working "With" a Relationship

In the next example, which illustrates the implementation of the relational model of treatment, the case manager also provides counseling for the client, R. R had been sober for one year following a 10-year period of alcohol and polydrug abuse. R was living with her 3 children and actively alcoholic husband. Her presenting problem was "depression." R could easily identify the source of her depression. She felt disconnected from her husband, a man with whom she had been in love for nine years. R was fearful that if she addressed her husband's drinking with him, he would leave her. The case manager validated R's love for her husband and explored the positive qualities in that relationship with R. It seemed to the case manager that the husband was very much in love with the client and that the relationship was in many respects a mutual, caring one. However, the client, because of her poor self-esteem, did not believe she could have any power in the relationship. For the next several sessions, the case manager and R role played the discussion that R would like to have with her husband. Eventually R became empowered to talk with her husband about the effect his drinking had on her. Her husband's response was quite positive and he has now been sober 14 months.

The case manager utilized the relational model to work with the strengths in R's relationship with her husband. Had she denigrated that relationship by recommending that R separate from her husband because her own sobriety was in jeopardy (as a traditional substance abuse treatment provider would), R would not have learned to take the risk of expressing her needs in the relationship, thereby taking it to another level of empathic contact and mutuality. In addition, suggesting to R that she leave her husband might well have resulted in her leaving treatment.

In this last example, the case manager's interventions are based upon the premise that empathy from and for others promotes empathy for the self. L, a women in early recovery, asserted that her drugging had not had any adverse effects on her children. She rationalized that her children were always fed and clothed, their medical care was attended to and they went to school every day. The case manager never challenged this perception (that is, did not confront the denial as a traditional substance abuse treatment provider might) but did work with L around understanding her addiction as a disease which often controls a person to such an extent that they behave in ways they never would have under any other circumstances. By taking this empathic stance, the case manager enabled L to develop empathy for her past self, the active addict. Eventually, L spontaneously admitted that she was terrified of facing the ways in which her behavior had adversely impacted her children. In fact, it turned out that every time her children had any sort of problem, no matter how remote the chances were that the problem was related to their mother's addiction, L would obsess about the possibility. By the time she got in touch with the shame and guilt she felt about the impact of her addiction upon her children, she was able to tolerate it because she could be empathic with her addicted self. The timing of L's ability to acknowledge these thoughts and feelings was crucial to her treatment. Had her denial been "confronted" earlier in her sobriety she probably would have been flooded with overwhelming feelings of guilt and shame, which might have led to relapse.

The relational model is still in the infancy stage of development and clearly needs more theoretical exploration, delineation of interventions, and research to distinguish it from other forms of treatment. However, this theoretical position has implications that impact staff members, not just clients.

For example, in this model, emotional ties between clients and staff are seen as mutual. In other words, relationships with clients are seen as growth promoting, not just for clients, but for staff members as well. Whether it is the strength received from working with a client who perseveres in spite of horrendous odds or a more direct thank-you as seen in the letter below, clients are continuously giving gifts. Acknowledging and appreciating these gifts make the work more rewarding.

Dear (Case Manager),

It was so nice for me to receive the card you sent while I was in detox. I want to thank you, and let you know that I have moved on to further treatment. I am in a half-way house. I have been here for a week now. It's not easy but I am giving it my best shot. I have been in treatment now for the last thirty-three days, and I'm feeling a little better. I hope to see you soon when I return back home. I am glad to have you as a part of my life and recovery. I hope to be hearing from you periodically.

Your friend,
M

The relational model also leads to the suggestion that relationships among staff members are of primary importance as sources of support and creative energy to promote professional and personal growth and prevent burnout. The experience of the staff of PSB has underlined the fact that activities such as staff meetings, individual and peer supervision, formal and informal case consultations and even having lunch together may be of more value than has been traditionally acknowledged and may need to be protected as much as possible from encroachment by client needs or attempts to utilize time more "efficiently." Female staff members may need to continuously rediscover that taking care of themselves is part of taking care of their clients.

Empowerment of staff members is important in a program which is designed to empower clients. The PSB staff receive great satisfaction from promoting change at the social policy level. They do this by feeding back what is learned from the clients and other service providers to those in power. This takes the form of education and advocacy work. Program staff are encouraged to participate in coalitions, national organizations and steering committees whose missions are to improve services for women and their children. They work with these organizations to plan conferences, public education events, and other activities which educate service providers and social policy makers about issues relevant to the special needs of women. Knowing that they are helping to change attitudes and policies that are adversely affecting clients helps offset the hopeless and helpless feelings that can be stimulated when working with a disenfranchised population. By impacting the system at various levels, staff members are not left with the feeling that they are simply applying bandaids. In addition, these activities foster professional growth by expanding knowledge and skills. And finally, these committees and coalitions provide another opportunity for obtaining support from colleagues.

The model also implies that the most effective process for refining strategies for engaging and retaining women clients in treatment would be one in which treatment providers meet and share experiences and perceptions with one another and use these as a basis for the development of ideas for clinical practice and for research. The present paper is the result of the staff of Project Second Beginning participating in such a process.

REFERENCES

Allison, M., & Hubbard, R. (1985). Drug abuse treatment process: A review of the literature. *International Journal of the Addictions, 20,* 1321-1345.

Aron, W.J., & Dailey, D.W. (1977). Graduates and splitees from therapeutic community drug treatment programs: A comparison. *The International Journal of the Addictions, 11,* 1-18.

Baekland, F., & Lundwall, L. (1975). Dropping out of treatment: A critical review. *Psychological Bulletin, 82,* 738-783.

Beck, N.C., Shekim, M.D., Fraps, C., Borgmeyer, A., & Whitt, A. (1983). Prediction of discharges against medical advice from a drug and alcohol misuse treatment program. *Journal of Studies on Alcohol, 39,* 491-498.

Beckman, L.J. (1978). The self-esteem of women alcoholics. *Journal of Studies on Alcohol, 39,* 491-498.

Beckman, L.J., & Amaro, H. (1984-85). Patterns of women's use of alcohol treatment agencies. *Alcohol and Research World, 9,* 14-25.

Beckman, L.J., & Bardsley, P.E. (1986). Individual characteristics, gender differences, and drop out from alcoholism treatment. *Alcohol and Alcoholism, 21* 213-244.

Brill, L. (1981). *The clinical treatment of substance abusers.* New York: The Free Press.

Chodorow, N. (1978). *The reproduction of mothering.* Berkeley: University of California Press.

Dahlgren, L., & Wilander, A. (1989). Are special treatment facilities for female alcoholics needed? A controlled two year follow up study from a specialized treatment unit (EWA) versus a mixed male/female treatment facility. *Alcoholism: Clinical and Experimental Research, 13,* 499-504.

Gilligan, C. (1982). *In a different voice: Psychological theory and women's development.* Cambridge, MA: Harvard University Press.

Greene, B.T., & Ryser, P.E. (1967). Impact of sex on length of time spent in treatment and treatment success. *American Journal of Drug and Alcohol Abuse, 5,* 97-105.

Harrison, P.A. (1989). Women in treatment: Changing over time. *The International Journal of the Addictions, 14,* 655-673.

Kaplan, A. (1984). *Female or male psychotherapists for women: New formulations.* Work in progress. Wellesley, MA: Wellesley College: Stone Center for Developmental Studies.

Miller, J.B. (1991). The development of women's sense of self. In J. Jordan, A. Kaplan, J. Miller, I. Stiver & J. Surrey (Eds.). *Women's growth in connection: Writings from the Stone Center.* New York: Guilford Press.

Mulford, H.A. (1977). Women and men problem drinkers: Sex differences in patients served by Iowa's community alcoholism centers. *Journal of Studies on Alcohol, 38,* 1624-1639.

Nichols, M. (1985). Theoretical concerns in the clinical treatment of substance abusing women: A feminist analysis. *Alcoholism Treatment Quarterly, 2,* 78-79.

Reed, B.G. (1985). Drug misuse and dependency in women: The meaning and implications of being considered a special population or minority group. *The International Journal of the Addictions, 20,* 13-62.

Root, M.P.P. (1989). Treatment failures: Role of sexual victimization in women's addictive behavior. *American Journal of Orthopsychiatry, 59,* 542-549.

Sandmaier, M. (1980). *The invisible alcoholics.* New York: McGraw-Hill.

Sansone, J. (1980). Retention patterns in a therapeutic community for the treatment of drug abuse. *The International Journal of the Addictions, 15,* 711-736.

Schilit, R., & Gomberg, E.S. (1987). Social support structures for women in treatment for alcoholism. *Health and Social Work, 12,* 187-195.

Schuckit, M.A. (1983). Alcoholism and other psychiatric disorders. *Hospital and Community Psychiatry, 34,* 1022-1027.

Simpson, P.D. (1979). Treatment for drug abuse: Follow-up outcomes and length of time spent. *Archives of General Psychiatry, 36,* 772-780.

Stark, M.J. (1992). Dropping out of substance abuse treatment: A clinically oriented review. *Clinical Psychology Review, 12,* 93-116.

Stark, M.J., & Campbell, B.K. (1988). Personality, drug use, and early attrition from substance abuse treatment. *American Journal of Drug and Alcohol Abuse, 14,* 475-487.

Steer, R.A. (1983). Retention in drug-free counseling. *The International Journal of the Addictions, 18,* 1109-1114.

Stevens, S., Arbiter, N., & Glider, P. (1989). Women residents: Expanding their role to increase treatment effectiveness in substance abuse programs. *The International Journal of the Addictions, 24,* 425-434.

Surrey, J.F. (1991). The "self-in-relation": A theory of women's development. In J. Jordan, A. Kaplan, J. Miller, I. Stiver & J. Surrey (Eds.). *Women's growth in connection: Writings from the Stone Center.* New York: Guilford Press.

Underhill, B.L. (1986). Issues relevant to aftercare programs for women. *Alcohol Health and Research World, Volume II, Fall.*

Wilson, B.L. (1991). Treatment for two. *Governing, July,* 37-41.

Yalom, I.D. (1985). *The theory and practice of group psychotherapy.* New York: Basic Books, Inc.

What Difference Does Culture Make?
Providing Treatment
to Women Different from You

Carmella H. Woll, MBA

SUMMARY. The United States is a country of people with culturally and ethnically diverse backgrounds. As no two cultures or two individuals are quite alike, the cultural differences and potential incompatibilities that the interactants bring to a specific encounter can add complexity to the counseling experience. Therefore, service providers in cross-cultural encounters must be able to meet the challenges of divergent and unfamiliar cultural experiences, behaviors and identities to achieve successful treatment outcomes.

This paper explores the concept of culture competency in substance abuse counseling with women of color. The term cultural competence is defined here as a set of academic and interpersonal skills that allow individuals to increase their understanding and appreciation of cultural differences and similarities within, among and between groups.

Generalizations about cultural groups will be used to illustrate the importance of cultural sensitivity in counseling women of color. These generalizations are not intended to stereotype or to imply that all women from the same cultural group are identical or approachable in exactly the same way, but are an attempt to stimulate awareness of cultural differences. *[Article copies available from The Haworth Document Delivery Service: 1-800-342-9678. E-mail address: getinfo@haworth.com]*

[Haworth co-indexing entry note]: "What Difference Does Culture Make? Providing Treatment to Women Different from You." Woll, Carmella H. Co-published simultaneously in *Journal of Chemical Dependency Treatment* (The Haworth Press, Inc.) Vol. 6, No. 1/2, 1996, pp. 67-85; and: *Chemical Dependency: Women at Risk* (ed: Brenda L. Underhill, and Dana G. Finnegan) The Haworth Press, Inc., 1996, pp. 67-85; and: *Chemical Dependency: Women at Risk* (ed: Brenda L. Underhill, and Dana G. Finnegan) Harrington Park Press, an imprint of The Haworth Press, Inc., 1996, pp. 67-85. Single or multiple copies of this article are available from The Haworth Document Delivery Service [1-800-342-9678, 9:00 a.m. - 5:00 p.m. (EST) E-mail address: getinfo@haworth.com].

INTRODUCTION

As far back as 1946 and 1947, Bales (1946) and Glad (1947) noted the differences between Irish and Jewish drinking behavior. Lolli and his colleagues (1958), studying drinking patterns in both Italian and French cultures in the Old World, confirmed that at least for the Italians, moderation in drink was rooted in cultural heritage.

Others who have focused on ethnic characteristics in drinking behavior among white males are Ullman (1958); Jellinek (1960); Sadoun, Lolli and Silverman (1965); and Knupfer and Room (1967). Although alcoholism research is one of the few areas in the social sciences that has considered issues of ethnic diversity, this research has focused primarily on ethnic groups among white males.

Like most medical research, collection of data reflecting the lives of women of color has been sorely neglected in studies of patterns of alcohol and other drug abuse. It would seem as if the lives of women of color have been too alien to comprehend or too far from sight to be included in the research for the planning and implementation of alcohol and other drug services.

Gender Differences

A major ongoing problem for the majority of women's programs and programs that serve women is their inability to honor and respect the complexity of women (particularly women of color) and the diversity of their lives. Although some researchers, such as Powell (1988) and Epstein (1988), have claimed that social norms and value differences between men and women are relatively minor, others (Henning & Jardim, 1976; Gilligan, 1982; and Helgesen, 1990) have argued successfully that they are quite significant. Some of the specific ways that different socialization affects women are in their different ways of learning and creating knowledge (Belenky, Clinchy, Goldberg, & Tarule, 1986) and in the way women play (Tannen, 1960).

Socialization of people in this society is segmented and distinct based greatly on gender; consequently, women hold a different worldview and experience life differently than men. Since the traditional roles society has defined for women and men produce quite different behavior, goals, self-images, and life experiences, women have a number of problems that are not relevant to men. Lack of self-esteem, stress, physiological issues, such as premenstrual tension and menopause, have been suggested as causes of women's drinking. If she fails at what her community or cultural environment has determined to be important (or what she perceives as important), she has failed as a woman. Sometimes, alcohol and other drug abuse help alleviate that failure.

While some programs may recognize and respond to the cultural significance of gender, the importance of cultural distinctions among racioethnic groups is frequently misunderstood and is often granted little validity in the actual practices of prevention, intervention and treatment of alcoholism and other drug abuse.

Racioethnic Differences

Since substance abuse doesn't discriminate according to race, class, sexual orientation or physical and mental abilities, neither should programs. Yet, many programs do not consider or make distinctions between client resistance based on such factors as racism, ethnocentrism, classism, and/or heterosexism, and resistance to change based on genuine personal disagreement or denial.

According to Chunn, Dunston, and Ross-Sheriff (1983), Loden and Rosener (1991), Pedersen (1987), and Schlesinger (1991), the failure of treatment programs to understand and address the lives of people of color, to a large degree, can be traced back to lack of training of the staff administrators, providers, and social workers. Often, little thought is given to ongoing education for substance abuse clinicians and few channels exist to identify potential for errors once clinicians have completed educational programs. The resulting lack of awareness and sensitivity may lead to labeling and scapegoating the client as noncompliant, "not ready" for treatment, passive aggressive, or unwilling to take responsibility when she appears resistant to program methods and strategies.

McGoldrick (1982) asserts that when service providers decide what the problem is and the behaviors associated with that problem without sufficient feedback from the client, it leads to systematic inattention to the client's perception of what is wrong and this can lead to noncompliance, dissatisfaction and poor treatment outcome. Perhaps the woman client believes that the professional care being offered is incompatible with her problem. Much of this "incompatibility" may be rooted in the opposing worldviews which the client and the provider have about what comprises the problem. One source of such incompatibility can lie within a person's culturally and ethnically determined perceptions of the problem and the course of treatment.

For example, traditional Native American Indians conceptualize the dynamics of alcohol consumption differently than westerners. Duran (1990) suggests that they perceive alcohol as a spiritual entity that has been very destructive to the tribes' ways of life, a perspective that interprets alcoholism as a spiritual illness as well as a psychological disturbance. Consequently, healing cannot occur just through education and behavior changes but also requires acknowledging the spiritual dis-ease of alcoholism and other drug abuse. One way to do this is to ask people about their spiritual beliefs. Asking questions about their spiritual history and current practices may provide information that can be useful for the treatment approach including people who may serve as part of the woman's support system during her recovery and healing.

Studies by Harwood (1981), Tseng and McDermott (1981), and Rakel (1977) have shown that people differ in:

1. their experience of pain
2. what they label as symptoms
3. how they communicate their pain or symptoms
4. their beliefs about the cause of illness
5. their attitudes toward helpers (counselors or doctors)
6. what treatment they want or expect.

And writers such as Sue and Sue (1990), Atkinson, Maryuma, and Matsui (1983), and Bryson and Bardo (1975) have clearly articulated that ethnic minorities do not particularly value "personal insight" or the ability to talk about the deepest and most intimate aspects of one's life–a point well worth consideration since the ability to self-disclose is a characteristic in counseling or therapy which is often seen as linked to a healthy personality.

PROBLEMS AND ISSUES

Lack of sensitivity to cultural issues sets the stage for service providers to minimize cultural differences by stressing the similarities between racial/ethnic groups. Statements such as, "We all have feelings," "I look at each person on an individual basis," "I see no color," "We're here to treat substance abuse, not to deal with differences," and "An addict is an addict" are often heard. Although these and other such statements may merit discussion in some situations, these points cannot and should not be used to negate cultural differences of tradition, customs, history, herstory, spiritual or religious practices and socioeconomic circumstances. Such statements express attitudes which demonstrate an inability or unwillingness of service providers to learn about and honor differences. If they hold such attitudes, professionals generally attempt to further justify their position by minimizing the role of culture.

It is essential that service providers make a commitment to continuing to learn about other cultures, to assessing a variety of communication styles, and to improving counseling methods to make them appropriate to different populations.

This task may be difficult for those who were trained in and adhere to a set of white European-male-based cultural values which are often used by society to define what's perceived as "normal." When providers base expectations for clients on these values, inadequate treatment for many, if not most, women of color often results. For example, institutional systems established to assist women can cause women of color to have crises about self-identity. Stress resulting from attempts to make cultural adjustments may lead African American women to question who they are as they become conscious of their reasons for treatment, and the personal insight from this identity crisis may conflict with advice from a provider who suggests they move to a different neighborhood, develop new relationships and/or leave their children.

In addition to the value of relationships African American women hold and are being asked to deny, change or relinquish, the racism that exists in this country doesn't afford African American women the mobility that is granted to members of the dominant culture. To select just one example, the African American woman has fewer resources and societal supports which means fewer alternatives to buffer her interface with a nonsupportive, frequently racist dominant society. Low pay, little or no healthcare, little or no affordable childcare, no job training, and lack of employment creates stress that is often unresolved because of the color of her skin.

Fundamental differences between providers' and clients' views of recovery and the recovery process are often determined by the sociocultural ethnic backgrounds between the provider and the client. The following summarizes some of the problems and solutions regarding such differences.

Providers enter the substance abuse field with culture-bound definitions of abuse and recovery. They bring with them distinct practices for the prevention and treatment of substance abuse which can then widen the gap between the cultural view of the provider of these services and the cultural perspective of women of color receiving services in substance abuse recovery programs.

Programmatic Issues

To assure that issues of cultural differences are included in program planning efforts, certain questions must be asked of the policy makers, the staff and the clients. The basic question is not *whether* services are biased but to *what degree* and in what ways. Failure to admit this bias and disregarding the values of ethnic groups of color have led to blaming the woman and lead her, her family and her community to see providers not as helpers but as agents of social oppression whose primary function is to assure conformance to western-European-white-male based cultural values. The answers can be gained from taking a critical look at the agency and asking questions such as: Why doesn't the program work naturally for everyone? What has to be done to allow it to do so? Will the cultural background and composition of the agency allow counselors and staff to take corrective action? If not, what fundamental changes need to be made?

The majority of the health and social problems facing women of color today have their roots in history. It is difficult to fully understand and appreciate the issues of contemporary life for women of color without becoming familiar with historical events. As noted by Espin (1987), hooks (1993), and Sue and Sue (1990), women of color in this country have emerged from a history of oppression, oppression that continues still into the '90s. As a result of stress related to living as women of color in predominantly White America, the struggle for women of color has included having to cope with sexism, racism, poverty and single parenthood and, consequently, it may be difficult for women of color to own yet another problem–alcohol and other drug abuse.

As hooks (1993) points out, the ways in which a woman of color continues to be devalued by the larger society affect her perception of herself, her relationships, her environment and her ability to maintain some semblance of order and balance in the midst of chaos and imbalance. The result is an overwhelming sense of powerlessness, which may generate an attitude of self-blame, generalized mistrust, feelings of alienation and guilt, lack of control, economic vulnerability and, ultimately, a sense of hopelessness. And to add to the complexity of these issues, Erikson (1959) has theorized that individuals in crisis situations experience a heightened awareness of their identities, undergoing what he calls a transitory, excessive identity consciousness. The precipitating crisis in this case could be the method of treatment–a process that may require the client to adapt to a new and unknowable way of life. An example of this is when values about family, language and behaviors, etc., are called into question by the provider. During this crisis women begin to discover beliefs and practices that they originally had no idea existed. Women who attempt to recover from alcohol and other drug abuse in a culture and/or community different from the one in which they grew up must learn new modes of communication, new beliefs and new styles of courtship, parenthood, marriage, maturation, aging, and dying for which they have had no preparation.

Some women will have an easier time than others in making adjustments to a change in lifestyle, behaviors and practices. Because some women of color tend to live in bicultural environments where their values and practices may be discrepant and contradictory, it is not uncommon for these women to maintain separate and distinct selves compatible with different cultures; behaviors and practices may change depending on the cultural situation. For example, a woman may be submissive to authority in one instance while confronting in another. These are some of the issues that must be addressed in prevention, intervention and treatment services that are being designed and operated for women of color if they are to be culturally sensitive and relevant.

METHODS AND STRATEGIES

In an age of diversity, such as this country is now experiencing, a process for working toward understanding multiculturalism needs to be developed for programs serving a variety of ethnic groups of color. The simple process presented in this article can be used as a guide for the development of a more comprehensive model. A first step is in the process of self awareness.

Self Awareness

Acting on one's own cultural values and traditions is as natural as breathing. It is so natural that a person usually is not aware of mannerisms and customs unique to one's own culture. What is taken for granted in one culture may seem strange to someone of another culture. The belief that one's own cultural ways are best is ethnocentrism. Providers need to intercept their own conscious or unconscious tendencies to be ethnocentric by acknowledging how their day-to-day behaviors have been shaped by cultural norms and values and have been reinforced by their families, peers and social institutions. Problems occur when those providing services to women of color assume the women share the same values as the provider.

Knowing one's own personal biases, values and interests which stem from culture will greatly enhance a person's sensitivity toward other cultures. Locke (1992) suggests that awareness of one's own culture is the first step to understanding others. The process of seeking that awareness can be facilitated by answering the following questions:

- What is my ethnicity?
- Who in my family most influenced my sense of ethnic identity?
- Who named me? Where did my name originate?
- What has my name meant to me over the years?
- How have others reacted to it? What was the family celebration I remember the most?
- How was alcohol used or not used in my family?
- At what age and under what circumstances did I take my first drink?

- How do you know when someone has drunk "too much"? (Be as specific as possible)
- Where do I go when I am in need of help?

Comparing responses to these questions from a diverse group of women can demonstrate how women from various cultures differ in their worldview and life experiences. There are many definitions of culture. The language and customs of a culture will influence whether or not a symptom is labeled as a problem. Cultures do not uniformly categorize conditions as disease or illness and vary in their beliefs regarding the cause, prevention, and treatment of disease and illness. An example of this is that for many traditional and/ or indigenous cultures the western notions of "mental illness" are not part of the belief system. In these cultures, disorders, which western society calls "mental illness," are perceived as spiritual disalignments or physically-based problems that can be treated and/ or cured by rituals or home healing practices.

Even when providers come from the same ethnic background as the women of color they serve, they may not share similar beliefs and values. In fact, Kleinman (1986) has noted that other factors like gender, class, education and occupational differences may make it particularly difficult to work with women who share the same ethnicity as the provider. For example, some programs mistakenly hire staff who are Spanish surnamed believing that this will make the staff compatible with a Southwestern U.S. Mexican American population. However, if the staff person is from Latin America or has a middle-class orientation, she may have little in common with U.S. working class Mexican American women. Moreover, being of the same ethnic or cultural group as the client may cause problems in some cases, as the provider's ethno-cultural identity may give rise to countertransference difficulties in providing services to women of color.

Countertransference occurs when the provider responds to a woman as he or she responded to someone in the past. And because providers prefer to see themselves as objective and empathetic to women of color, they may unconsciously establish a dysfunctional pattern of interaction in this relationship. Some countertransference issues affecting the treatment of African American women are prejudicial judgments made by the provider regarding the suitability of the client for therapy due to a perceived passiveness or resistance on the part of the client. Guilt may also make white providers reluctant to address or even admit the African American woman's hostility toward them. The expression of aggression among African Americans is often repressed and leads to a heightened anxiety. In addition, a provider may inappropriately identify with an alcohol or other drug abusing woman who is well-dressed, well-educated and married. Identification with this client could result in efforts to mentor the woman rather than provide the counseling that will address the client's need for recovery. Such conflicts get played out in therapy in subtle and not so subtle ways that can be destructive to the process of treatment.

It is important to note that cultural factors in and of themselves do not create transference or countertransference. But all people are shaped by cultural factors to respond in particular ways in particular situations. Thus, issues from a woman's past can be exacerbated by having a therapist from a different culture who has no understanding or knowledge of the influence of this particular cultural factor on a woman's life. An example of this is family cultural practices, such as female circumcision among some African American clients.

Providers need to acknowledge how their day-to-day behaviors have been shaped by cultural norms and values and have been reinforced by their families, peers and social institutions. How one defines family, health, and illness and how one determines life goals, articulates problems, and even says "hello" are influenced by the culture in which one functions. Providers knowledgeable about alcoholism and other drug abuse need to become more aware of how dynamic cultural patterns influence use, abuse, addiction and the recovery process.

In addition to self-awareness, providers need to have some knowledge and information about the groups to whom they intend to provide services. The second step in the process of achieving competency in cross-cultural counseling is to gain an understanding of values systems in other cultures and their influence on recovery from alcohol and other drugs. Every culture has a value system that dictates behavior directly or indirectly in that it sets norms and teaches that those norms are correct. Beliefs and practices about wellness and illness reflect that value system.

Models for Describing the Effects of Sociocultural Elements of Diversity

Sue and Sue (1990) are among those who have developed a model (see Figure 1) that emphasizes the impact of sociocultural factors in addition to the psychological and developmental influences on different groups of people of color.

There are many elements of culture to examine in the model presented here. The primary ones–racial factors, gender issues, age,

FIGURE 1. Model Depicting the Elements of Diversity

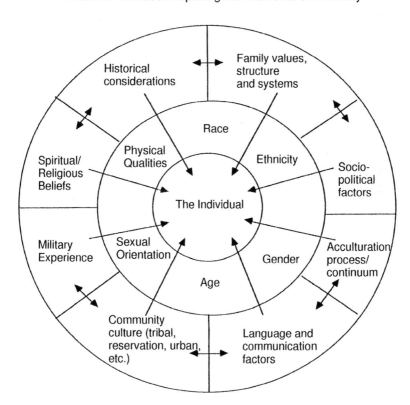

sexual orientation, ethnicity and physical qualities–are indicated in the middle circle. The secondary ones–sociopolitical factors, linguistic abilities, religious/spiritual beliefs, degree of acculturation, family values, structures and systems, herstory of oppression, military experience and community culture–are represented in the outer circle. Knowledge of these elements forms the core of the information necessary to provide services that are culturally relevant.

For example, knowledge about a woman's home country, its political climate, and its historical evolution may explain why she left, what occupation she held, and the cultural expectations of women. This information allows the provider to see beyond the client's immigrant status, with its inherent limitations, to her strengths and resources. As a result, more appropriate and relevant interventions can be planned.

Elements of Diversity

Primary Elements

The primary elements in this model are those immutable differences that are inborn and/or exert an important impact on the early socialization of a woman and have an ongoing impact throughout her life. Race, ethnicity, gender, age, physical qualities, and sexual orientation are the primary factors that serve as the core of who she is as an individual. These factors are central to her life and serve as the filters for her life experiences. What she sees and experiences cannot be separated from these factors because her thoughts, feelings and behaviors are inextricably linked to them. The perspective of women of color about who they are is built on these primary elements.

Providers must not consider only those elements relating to the experiences in the present but must learn about those events from the past or future that may have an impact on the present. For some women of color it is a recollection of the past that contributes to their willingness or unwillingness to seek or participate in treatment.

Secondary Elements

Family values, sociopolitical factors, the acculturation process, language, community culture, military experience, spiritual/religious beliefs and historical considerations make up the secondary elements. This list, however, may include other aspects, such as class, economics and education. The elements listed as secondary can be changed by what the client sees and experiences in her life. They add breadth and contour to her self-definition as some of them recede and change over time while others remain permanently.

Acculturation/assimilation serves as a prime example of those changes. When assessing the level of acculturation providers need to consider marital, attitudinal, behavioral, structural and identification factors. A major difference is the degree to which they have immersed themselves in the mainstream culture. Not only will women of color vary in their participation and response to acculturation, some domains of culture and behavior may become altered with comparable changes in other domains. As individuals interact with others different from themselves, there is the opportunity for learning, teaching and change. That is, the acculturation process is an uneven one and does not affect all cultural phenomena in a uniform manner.

Furthermore, not all women of color want to be absorbed into the dominant culture and some will be resistant to attempts at changing their behaviors "to fit in." For example, many women of color in early treatment resist the treatment because it is perceived as an attempt to "assimilate" them into the dominant culture and pull them away from that which is safe and familiar to them. For these women, recovery is much more difficult because there is much pressure from the environment, including family and friends, to remain a part of the culture.

The interplay among both primary and secondary elements shapes each woman's worldview, priorities, values and behaviors.

Integration Through Application

When a provider does not possess the necessary knowledge about a particular group receiving services, then consultation or training to learn information or referral to someone more knowledgeable may be appropriate. Service providers have an ethical obligation and a social responsibility to respect cultural and individual differences. No one can know everything about everybody and each person must recognize personal limitations.

Cultural assessments are necessary in planning recovery services because the information obtained can identify patterns of belief and customs that can help or hinder recovery plans. Unless the provider is able to explain the relevance and importance of a thorough assessment and assure the woman of confidentiality, incomplete data is more likely to be given.

Assessment is a clinical art that combines sensitivity, clinical judgment, cultural awareness, and scientific knowledge. Not only must one know when to ask questions, but also how to phrase them so that the woman does not find them offensive. For example, asking a woman of color what her ethnic identity is may not be a good idea. One reason for this is that like most members of the dominant culture, she may not have thought much about this issue because it's just who she is. If, however, the provider instead asks, "Where are you from?" and learns more about her background, the provider can learn about her ethnic identity over time. Another reason for resistance may be fear of retribution if that information is revealed. Women's history around the world includes many examples of atrocities inflicted upon them because they were not of the particular ethnic group in power.

Cultural Assessment Stages

It is not feasible to do a complete cultural assessment for every woman who enters a program. Nor is it possible to do a complete assessment in a single visit. The use of this assessment tool may be utilized during many different phases of client contact. Some aspects can be easily integrated into the standard or initial client interview or meeting. It may be more appropriate in certain situations to forego some questions until a therapeutic alliance has been forged. Timing needs to be dictated by the situation. The following three-stage approach can be integrated into an existing process, keeping in mind that the initial visit is extremely important and can determine whether or not the woman returns.

In the first stage, background information can be collected on:

- Ethnicity
- Degree of affiliation with the ethnic group
- Spiritual/Religious beliefs

- Decision making processes
- Additional factors that may influence the relationship between the provider and the woman (e.g., language, style of communication, expectations).

In collecting the information during the first stage, asking questions about ethnicity can provide the provider with clues about particular ethnic/cultural patterns of thinking and behaving.

- Is this person a recent immigrant, refugee, first generation? How acculturated is this person?
- Are there religious/spiritual beliefs and/or practices that need to be included in the recovery plan? Spirituality for some ethnic groups is the essence of being healthy.
- Who else needs to be included in the decisions to be made? Collectivism (emphasis on family, tribe or community) is a value in some ethnic groups. The determination to stay clean and sober may depend on the involvement of others.
- What communication patterns should the provider respect, such as how a woman wants to be addressed, eye contact, touching, tone of voice, distance between persons, modesty considerations, avoiding terms that could be misunderstood (e.g., enabling, codependency, alcoholism) and expected expressiveness (silence, high verbal vs. low verbal context, etc.)?

Determining Culture Specific Views

In the second stage, it is important to determine the culture-specific view of the woman who seeks recovery:

- What caused her to seek services?
- What does she define as the "problem"?
- What does she think caused the "problem"?
- Who does she usually talk to when she is in trouble?
- What has she already tried to do to take care of herself?
- What does she expect to happen and what does she want the results to be?
- What fears does she have about receiving services?
- What life problems does she associate with her requiring services?

The third stage identifies the cultural patterns that can help or hinder the provision of services:

- Who in her family has she talked to about seeking services?
- Who else has she talked to?
- What does she think she needs to do?
- Who does she consider to be a part of her support system?
- What does she think needs to happen for her to continue receiving services?

The information gathered in these stages enables the provider to determine who the support people and resources are that are trusted, utilized by and available to the client. Incorporation of these resources into the treatment or recovery plan can support the woman while receiving services as well as after termination of services from the provider.

The reader is encouraged to explore some of the resource materials available for providers about being sensitive to racial, class, and minority issues in counseling (e.g., Brislen, 1990; Devore & Schlesinger, 1991; Logan, 1981; McGoldrick, Pearce & Giordano, 1982; Pedersen, 1987; Sue & Sue, 1991). Additionally, information is becoming increasingly available in such journals as the *Journal of Cross-Cultural Psychology* and the *International Journal of Psychology*. While these sources rarely address gender issues directly, other resources, Blea (1992); Boyd (1993); Farley (1993); Green (1992); hooks (1993); Perrone, Stockel and Kruger (1989); Soto (1990); and the Women's South Asian Collective (1994), are available to help the provider better understand how women's lives, strengths, problems, and expectations of themselves and others may vary depending on their culture.

CONCLUSION

Through heightened awareness and understanding of cultural contexts, the provider can do much to meet the challenge of ethnocentrism. Remaining open to the wide range of cultural possibilities can be very difficult for a service provider. The ambiguity can be threatening and cause an emotional shutdown when providers are confronted with too many differences.

Cross-cultural counseling presents a challenge because it requires service providers to work with women of color without making judgments as to the superiority or rightness of one set of values over another. What can make a difference in this issue is not eradicating cultural differences but developing their potential to become a source of cultural enrichment.

The need is for increased sensitivity to culture as learned behavior, increased information about women of specific cultures, embedded subcultures and ethnic groups, as well as an emphasis on actual value systems and clashes between and within value systems. All of these can markedly increase the capacity of the provider to work productively with clients who are women of color.

> Difference is that raw and powerful connection from which our personal power is forged.

—Audre Lorde

NOTE

Special thanks are extended to Dr. Juana Mora for her invaluable assistance with the editing of this article, which was greatly appreciated by the author, now deceased.

REFERENCES

Atkinson, D.R., Maruyama, M., & Matsui, S. (Eds.). (1983). *Counseling American minorities: A cross-cultural perspective.* Iowa: W. C. Brown.

Bales, R.F. (1946). Cultural differences in rates of alcoholism. *Quarterly Journal of Studies on Alcohol, 6,* 480-99.

Belenky, M.F., Clinchy, B.M., Goldberg, N.R., & Tarule, J.M. (Eds.). (1986). *Women's ways of knowing.* New York: Basic Books.

Blea, I. (1992). *La Chicana and the intersection of race, class, and gender.* New York: Praeger.

Boyd, J.A. (1988). (Unpublished ms.) Advanced Feminist Therapy Institute Conference. Seattle.

Boyd, J.A. (1993). *In the company of sisters: Black women and self-esteem.* New York: Penguin.

Brislin, R.W. (1990). *Applied cross-cultural psychology.* Beverly Hills, CA: Sage.

Bryson, S., & Bardo, H. (1975). Race and the counseling process: An Overview. *Journal of Non-White Concerns in Personnel and Guidance, 4*(1), 5-15.

Chunn, J.C., Dunston, P.J. & Ross-Sheriff, F. (Eds.). (1983). *Mental health & people of color.* Washington, DC: Howard University Press.

Devore, W., & Schlesinger, E.G. (Eds.). (1991). *Ethnic-sensitive social work practice.* New York: Macmillan.

Duran, E. (1990). *Transforming the soul wound.* Berkeley: Folklore Institute.

Epstein, C.F. (1988). *Deceptive distinctions; Sex, gender and the social order.* New York: Yale University Press.

Erikson, E.H. (1959). *Identity and the life cycle.* New York: Norton.

Espin, O.M. (1987). Handbook of cross-cultural counseling and therapy. *Psychotherapy with hispanic women.* New York: Greenwood Press.

Farley, A. (1993). *Women of the native struggle.* New York: Orion Books.

Gilligan, C. (1982). *In a different voice: Psychological theory and women's development.* Cambridge: Harvard University Press.

Glad, D.C. (1947). Attitudes and experiences of American-Jewish and American-Irish male youth as related to differences in adult rates of inebriety. *Quarterly Journal of Studies of Alcohol, 8,* 406-72.

Greeley, A.M., McCready, W.C., & Theisen, G. (Eds.). (1980). *Ethnic drinking subcultures.* New York: Greenwood Press.

Green, R. (1992). *Women in American Indian society.* New York: Chelsea House.

Harwood, A. (1981). *Ethnicity and medical care.* Cambridge: Harvard University Press.

Helgesen, S. (1990). *The female advantage: Women's ways of leadership.* New York: Doubleday.

hooks, B. (1993). *Sisters of the yam: Black women and self-recovery.* Boston: South End Press.

Kleinman, A. (1980). *Patients and healers in the context of culture.* Berkeley: University of California Press.

Knupfer, G., & Room, R. (1967). Drinking patterns and attitudes of Irish, Jewish, and white Protestant American men. *Quarterly Journal of Studies on Alcohol, 28,* 676-99.

Locke, D. (1992). *Increasing multicultural understanding.* California: Sage Publications.

Loden, M., & Rosener, J.B. (1991). *Workforce America! Managing employee diversity as a vital resource.* Illinois: Business One.

Lolli, G.E. , Serianni, G.M., & Luzzato-Fegiz, P. (Eds.). (1958). *Alcohol in American Italian culture.* Piscataway, NJ: Rutgers University Center of Alcohol Studies.

Lustig, W., & Koester, J. (1993). *Intercultural competence.* New York: Harper-Collins.

McGoldrick, M., Pearce, J.K., & Giordano, J. (Eds.). (1982). *Ethnicity and family therapy.* New York: Guilford Press.

Pedersen, P. (1987). *Handbook of cross-cultural counseling and therapy.* New York: Greenwood Press.

Perrone, B., Stockel, H.H., & Krueger, U. (Eds.). (1989). *Medicine women, curanderas, and women doctors.* Oklahoma: University Press.

Rakel, R.E. (1977). *Principles of family medicine.* Philadelphia: Saunders.

Sadoun, A., Lolli, G., & Silverman, M. (1965). *Drinking in French culture.* Piscataway, NJ: Rutgers University Center of Alcohol Studies.

Soto, S. (1990). *Emergence of the modern Mexican woman.* Denver: Arden Press.

Sue, D.E., & Sue D. (1990). *Counseling the culturally different* (3rd ed.). New York: John Wiley & Sons.

Tannen, D. (1990). *You just don't understand: Women and men in conversation.* New York: William Morrow.

Ting-Toomey, S., & Korzenny, F. (1991). *Cross-cultural interpersonal communication.* Newbury Park, CA: Sage.

Tseng, W.S., & McDermott, J.F. (1981). *Culture, mind, and therapy: An introduction to cultural psychiatry.* New York: Brunner/Mazel.

Women of South Asian Descent Collective. (1994). *Our feet walk the sky: Women of the South Asian diaspora.* San Francisco: aunt lute books.

Zola, I.K. (1972). The concept of trouble and sources of medical assistance. *Social Science and Medicine, 6,* 673-80.

Chemically Dependent Lesbians and Bisexual Women: Recovery from Many Traumas

Dana G. Finnegan, PhD, CAC
Emily B. McNally, PhD, CAC

INTRODUCTION

Lesbian and bisexual women[1] who are trying to recover from the destructive effects of both chemical dependency and homophobia/heterosexism face formidable problems and tasks. In addition, many such women must struggle with other forces such as the devastating effects of terrible emotional/physical neglect or physical and/or sexual abuse, often inflicted within a chaotic chemically dependent family system.

Unfortunately, long after they begin their recovery from chemical dependency and their process of developing a sense of self, many women are still beset by problems and issues which have neither improved substantially nor been resolved as a result of being clean and sober. Many lesbian and bisexual women with long-term[2] recovery are still plagued by such major problems as eating disorders, dissociative disorders, depression, Post-Traumatic Stress Disorder (PTSD), compulsive debting/spending, sexual dysfunction, inability to be intimate, relationship problems, internalized homophobia, sexual

[Haworth co-indexing entry note]: "Chemically Dependent Lesbians and Bisexual Women: Recovery from Many Traumas." Finnegan, Dana G., and Emily B. McNally. Co-published simultaneously in *Journal of Chemical Dependency Treatment* (The Haworth Press, Inc.) Vol. 6, No. 1/2, 1996, pp. 87-107; and: *Chemical Dependency: Women at Risk* (ed: Brenda L. Underhill, and Dana G. Finnegan) The Haworth Press, Inc., 1996, pp. 87-107; and: *Chemical Dependency: Women at Risk* (ed: Brenda L. Underhill, and Dana G. Finnegan) Harrington Park Press, an imprint of The Haworth Press, Inc., 1996, pp. 87-107. Single or multiple copies of this article are available from The Haworth Document Delivery Service [1-800-342-9678, 9:00 a.m. - 5:00 p.m. (EST) E-mail address: getinfo@haworth.com].

87

identity confusion, and self-harming behaviors. Having to struggle with such powerful problems can put these women in danger of relapse and negatively affect the quality of their lives.

Why so many lesbian and bisexual women with long-term recovery must battle with such difficult, complex, and painful circumstances; how they do so; and what life and treatment strategies may help them win this battle constitute the primary focus of this article.

One major source of understanding about this phenomenon of long-term recovery problems is the trauma literature and theory. Not until the last fifteen years has much been written about trauma— what it is, who it happens to, what its effects are, what its treatment is. Especially within the past ten years, more and more has been written. Reasons for this surge in research, the development of theory, and treatment approaches are various. The effects of their war experiences upon Vietnam veterans have become better known and understood; long-term work with and studies of Holocaust survivors have yielded much information about and greater understanding of trauma; there has been more attention to the psychology of being held hostage; and the Women's Movement has had an enormously powerful influence on our awareness and comprehension of the traumas of physical violence, rape, and sexual abuse.

Just what *is* trauma? Herman (1992) defines psychological trauma as

> an affliction of the powerless. At the moment of trauma, the victim is rendered helpless by overwhelming force. When the force is that of nature, we speak of disasters. When the force is that of other human beings, we speak of atrocities. Traumatic events overwhelm the ordinary systems of care that give people a sense of control, connection, and meaning. (p. 33)

McCann and Pearlman (1990)

> define psychological trauma as follows: An experience is traumatic if it (1) is sudden, unexpected, or non-normative, (2) exceeds the individual's perceived ability to meet its demands, and (3) disrupts the individual's frame of reference and other central psychological needs and related schemas. (p. 10)

It is possible to take these definitions and apply them to those conditions which are ordinarily not viewed as traumas–alcoholism, sexism, and homophobia. According to Bean (1981), addiction to mood-altering chemicals (including alcohol) often severely traumatizes the addicted person. If the addicted person is a woman, then she is subjected to at least one other kind of trauma, that of the threats of violence and the actual violence inherent in sexism (Herman, 1992). Furthermore, being a woman, her chances of being sexually abused are one in three (Herman, 1992). If this woman is also lesbian or bisexual, then she will experience the traumas inflicted by heterosexism, homophobia, and homo-hatred (Alvarez, 1994; Dillon, 1993; Finnegan & McNally, 1987, 1990; Hall, 1990a; Pharr, 1988). Common and frequent–if not inevitable–responses to these traumas are dissociation, depression, anxiety, shame and guilt, impairment of affect tolerance, psychosomatic conditions, and compulsions which are an acting out of feelings and internal conflicts.

Treating lesbians and bisexual women who are chemically dependent, therefore, is a task of major and complex proportions, made even more complex by such factors as the woman's stage of recovery, especially as it pertains to relapse potential; her stage of development of lesbian or bisexual identity; her family history; her history–if any–of physical, emotional and/or sexual abuse; the strength and nature of her psychological defenses; and the extent of her support systems.

MULTIPLE TRAUMAS

The lesbian or bisexual woman who is a recovering alcoholic has been subjected to at least three traumas. Bean (1981) likens alcoholism to other traumas such as being a concentration camp victim or being a survivor of a natural disaster. She describes the similarities as follows:

> In all these other events the painful process is experienced as unavoidable and overwhelming. There seems to be no explanation for it and no help for it. The psychological reactions to these traumas usually include a period of shock, decompensation, and regression. Then the person makes a variety of efforts to control, master, cope with, and later to bear, understand, and transcend the suffering. *That a person faced with*

the experience of alcoholism would react like other human beings faced with trauma seems obvious [Our italics]. That such a psychology of response to suffering must be understood to work effectively with alcoholics also seems clear. (p. 57)

She notes also that alcoholism is a

catastrophic experience–terrible losses, deprivations, the sense of being at hazard, shame and the certainty one can never atone, the ruin of self-esteem, the utter loss of hope. The alcoholic's circumstances are now wholly traumatic, and he/[she] must make a desperate effort to create a psychology for emotional survival. Denial under these conditions is a primitive defense invoked to stave off psychological collapse. (p. 90)

Thus the person who struggles with alcoholism is traumatized and must deal with the various attendant effects.

One trauma would be more than enough to deal with, but the alcoholic lesbian or bisexual woman must contend with *at least* two others. As Herman (1992) points out, "violence is a routine part of women's sexual and domestic lives" (p. 28); sexism as manifested by sexual threat and violence harms *all* women. She further states that "Not until the women's liberation movement of the 1970s was it recognized that the most common post-traumatic disorders are not those of men in war but of women in civilian life" (p. 28). Thus because she is a woman in this culture, the lesbian or bisexual woman is inevitably exposed to the traumatizing effects of sexism.

In addition, because of her sexual orientation, the lesbian or bisexual woman must deal with the trauma inflicted by homophobia and heterosexism. Alvarez (1994) contends that gay people[3] are very often victims of emotional, and often physical, abuse from our culture and likens them to Holocaust and sexual abuse survivors. Dillon (1993) speaks of "the malevolent influence of homophobia so evident in national life today . . ." (p. 1). We, the authors, agree that homophobia/homo-hatred is enormously destructive and trau- matizing. Gay people are the casualties of a vast range of abuses— from "gay-bashing" to vicious name-calling to rejection by family and friends. They are threatened with and subjected to physical

violence, emotional abuse, and spiritual rape if they do not con-
form, keep quiet, stay in the closet and thereby deny their identity,
negate their truths, and invalidate their Selves. What is demanded of
them is that they collude with their perpetrators. The demoralization
created by this action alone is enough to traumatize anyone.

To further compound the problem, many alcoholic lesbian and
bisexual women are adult children of alcoholics (ACOAs) who
have grown up in dysfunctional alcoholic family systems. In addition, according to Russell (1984), *one out of three women has been
sexually abused before the age of eighteen,* the majority of them in
their family. Herman (1992) powerfully describes the kind of childhood resulting from growing up in such dysfunctional circumstances:

> Chronic childhood abuse takes place in a familial climate of
> pervasive terror, in which ordinary caretaking relationships
> have been profoundly disrupted. Survivors describe a charac-
> teristic pattern of totalitarian control, enforced by means of
> violence and death threats, capricious enforcement of petty
> rules, intermittent rewards, and destruction of all competing
> relationships through isolation, secrecy, betrayal. . . . In addi-
> tion to the fear of violence, survivors consistently report an
> overwhelming sense of helplessness. In the abusive family
> environment, the exercise of parental power is arbitrary, capri-
> cious, and absolute. (p. 98)

Such a climate of terror inevitably traumatizes its young victims
and leaves them with scars for a lifetime.

THE EFFECTS OF MULTIPLE TRAUMAS

Herman (1992) has developed a schema which presents the characteristics of a new, more complete diagnostic entity–Complex
Post-Traumatic Stress Disorder–to describe the effects, or sequelae,
of subjection to totalitarian control, including childhood physical
and/or sexual abuse. We will use this schema in conjunction with
other writers' views to talk about some of the sequelae of trauma as
they apply particularly to people traumatized by alcoholism and

homophobia. A caveat is in order here. An examination of the ways various traumas affect people must recognize that there are significant differences between traumas such as, for example, childhood sexual abuse and alcoholism. Nevertheless, we want to present an inclusive view of the devastation wrought by all of these traumas in order to get a clearer look at the factors which affect the long-term recovery process of a lesbian or bisexual woman.

Totalitarian Control

Herman's (1992) first criterion is

A history of subjection to totalitarian control over a prolonged period (months to years). Examples include . . . those subjected to totalitarian systems in sexual and domestic life. . . . (p. 121)

We contend that not only childhood physical/sexual abuse but also the abuses of sexism and homophobia constitute totalitarian systems in women's sexual and domestic lives, enforcing their controls via terror, shame, and stigma.

Alterations in Affect Regulation

The second criterion is "Alterations in affect regulation, including [among others] persistent dysphoria [and] chronic suicidal preoccupation" (p. 121). Such dysphoria and suicidality are frequently evident in the course of people's alcoholism. Furthermore, women in this society often suffer from depression, almost as a matter of course. In addition, Herman (1992) cites "self injury" which can take many forms, one of which is substance abuse. Both she and Krystal (1988) speak also of the disruption of self-care, a phenomenon that Khantzian (1981) and Mack (1981) discuss as central to the devastation of alcoholism. Substance abuse as a means of dealing with the trauma of homophobia has often been cited as a major problem afflicting the gay/lesbian population (Finnegan & McNally, 1987; Hall, 1990a & b; McKirnan & Peterson, 1989a & b; Ziebold & Mongeon, 1985). And certainly in ongoing recovery such behaviors as eating disorders, self-mutilation, impulsive risk-taking, debting, compulsive sexual behavior are both problems and "solutions" because they "serve the function of regulating intolerable feeling states, in the absence of more adaptive self-soothing strategies" (Herman, 1992: p. 166).

Krystal (1988) also writes about the problems of affect regulation experienced by survivors of trauma, among them anhedonia and alexithymia, comprised in part by an "inability for reflective self-awareness (which enables one to identify one's 'feeling' as being an appropriate response to one's self-evaluation)" (p. 244). This inability to self-reflect and self-evaluate can play a significant role in a person's alcoholism, in that she cannot link emotion to act or emotion to meaning. Furthermore, this inability can create serious difficulties and obstacles in a person's attempts to develop a positive lesbian or bisexual identity in the face of severe oppression.

Krystal (1988) goes on to note that trauma survivors suffer from

> a posttraumatic impairment of affect tolerance because they experience their own emotions as *heralds of trauma* [Our italics]. Past that, one encounters the problems of alexithymia. The survivors try to block the distress by the use of medication [alcohol and/or drugs in the case of addiction] and keep "proposing a physical illness" (Balint, 1964) instead of utilizing their emotions as signals. (pp. 237-238)

This inability to use one's emotions as signals is an impairment common to alcoholism and can also be observed in lesbians or bisexual women with incompletely formed sexual-affectional identities. For example, a woman who is ambivalent or in conflict about her sexual-affectional identity may be so frightened of the possibility of being a lesbian that she will deny any emotional and/or sexual responses she experiences and thus be unable to utilize her emotions as signals of whatever her sexual orientation may be.

Alterations in Consciousness

Among the effects of trauma on consciousness listed are those of amnesia, transient dissociative episodes, and depersonalization-derealization (Herman, 1992). The trauma of active alcoholism most certainly produces dissociative episodes in the form of blackouts and brownouts. Recovery from alcoholism is often marked by what appear to be dissociative episodes (e.g., "The last thing I remember, I was walking by the bar and then all of a sudden I was sitting at the bar drinking. I don't know how that happened.") Krystal (1988) talks about "psychic numbing" that trauma survivors experience, in which they "are able to observe and describe the blocking of affective responses" (p. 151) and thus function while not feeling. Gay people who are subjected to the constant, ongoing totalitarian system of societal and familial homophobia intensified by their own personal, internalized homophobia learn to survive this emotional battering by "numbing out." They often don't hear (at least not on a conscious level) the homophobic jokes and slurs and innuendoes and whispers. They often don't see the looks, the gestures, the turning away. But to achieve this state, they may dissociate, unconsciously splitting off a part of themselves and keeping it separate and alone.

Alterations in Self-Perception

Three of the major characteristics Herman (1992) cites in this category are a "sense of helplessness"; "shame, guilt, and self-blame"; and a "sense of defilement or stigma" (p. 121). Certainly people who struggle with alcoholism and with the oppression of homophobia experience a sense of helplessness and concomitant despair. And, unfortunately, some degree of shame, guilt, and self-blame are the inevitable feeling states of those afflicted by alcoholism and/or homophobia. A sense of defilement or stigma is unavoidable in the face of societal disgust and hatred both for those who are alcoholic and for those who are lesbian or gay or bisexual. It should be noted also that people who are ACOAs often suffer from these same sequelae.

A fourth characteristic listed is a "sense of complete difference from others (may include sense of specialness, utter aloneness, belief no other person can understand, or nonhuman identity)" (Herman, 1992: p. 121). The despairing sense of complete and totally unacceptable difference from others captures the utter despair of the alcoholic who feels cast into outer darkness, not fit for human company. And many lesbian, gay, and bisexual people struggle from an early age with powerful feelings of difference and the strong belief (often accurate) that no other person can understand (or accept) their sexual orientation. In the face of vicious homophobia, it is difficult for many gays and bisexuals not to feel that they, too, have been cast into outer darkness.

Alterations in Perception of Perpetrator

Two characteristics in particular speak to the destructive effects of both alcoholism and homophobia–an "unrealistic attribution of total power to [the] perpetrator" and an "acceptance of [the] belief system or rationalizations of [the] perpetrator" (Herman, 1992: p. 121). In regard to the first, Herman (1992) adds a caution: "victim's assessment of power realities may be more realistic than clinician's" (p. 121). Certainly, the *feeling belief* active alcoholics usually hold is that alcohol has total power over them in the sense that they cannot live without it (while, paradoxically, believing at the same time that they can stop any time they choose). The First Step of Alcoholics Anonymous addresses this paradox by teaching alcoholics that while they are powerless over the *chemical effects* of alcohol, they have power (control) over their behavior. Many lesbians and bisexual women ascribe total (or a great deal of) power to society, living in fear of being "found out" and being shamed and rejected.

The second characteristic, accepting the belief system of the perpetrator, applies to alcoholics in a particular way. In and of itself, alcoholism, "the perpetrator," does not have a belief system; yet an internal belief system about the power and importance of alcohol develops within the alcoholic which then acquires the force of immutable reality. For example, many alcoholics are absolutely convinced that they cannot function, socialize, or even live without alcohol. Lesbians and bisexual women are subjected to society's shaming and threatening belief system that they are "unnatural," "sick," "sinful" freaks of nature, that they are failed heterosexuals. They accept these beliefs and/or are affected by them in proportion to how developed their sexual-affectional identity is. But no matter how advanced their identity development is, they are still subjected to the full weight of the cruel and often loudly proclaimed beliefs that society puts forth.

Alterations in Relations with Others

Davies and Frawley (1994) describe survivors' reenactments in adult relationships of the dynamics of the trauma of sexual abuse and the disruptive effects of those interactions. All of the conditions that Herman (1992) cites in this category are unnervingly familiar to anyone who knows alcoholism: "isolation and withdrawal; disruption in intimate relationships; repeated search for rescuer; persistent distrust; repeated failures of self-protection" (Herman, 1992: p. 121). These occur during a person's active alcoholism, but they continue far into a person's recovery (Bean, 1981; Khantzian, 1981). For the lesbian or bisexual woman, these conditions can mark major problems created by the trauma of homophobia. If women feel threatened because of their sexual-affectional orientation, they may indeed isolate and withdraw. Being lesbian or bisexual presents them with having to choose between keeping their orientation secret—an action which is destructive to close relationships—or coming out to others which puts them at risk of rejection. Either way, keeping secrets or coming out can and frequently does cause disruption in intimate relationships. And, certainly, the battering of homophobia can engender persistent distrust.

Alterations in Systems of Meaning

This category is marked by a "loss of sustaining faith [and a] sense of hopelessness and despair" (Herman, 1992: p. 121). For active alcoholics, these conditions are nearly inevitable. Recovery often involves an active struggle to regain faith and restore hope (Bean, 1981; Kurtz & Ketcham, 1992). In the face of virulent homophobia, it becomes extremely difficult for lesbians and bisexual women to sustain their faith in the societal system which makes up their cultural context. And in the face of society's betrayal of them, many lesbians and bisexual women fall prey to hopelessness and despair.

Physiological Effects

There is one other category which needs to be considered—that of physiological effects. That abuse has physiological effects is not in question. Krystal (1988) notes that when a person is alexithymic and cannot describe or express her affects, she may well express them through somatic symptoms. Van der Kolk (1987), Courtois (1988), and Herman (1992), among others, clearly describe the physiological effects of trauma. As Herman (1992) comments,

> Chronically traumatized people no longer have any baseline state of physical calm or comfort. Over time, they perceive their bodies as having turned against them. They begin to complain, not only of insomnia and agitation, but also of numerous types of somatic symptoms. Tension headaches, gastrointestinal disturbances, and abdominal, back, or pelvic pain are extremely common. Survivors may complain of tremors, choking sensations, or rapid heartbeat. (p. 86)

Both Courtois (1988) and Herman (1992) describe the self-harming behaviors which can have long-term somatic consequences, such as "chronic suicidality, self-mutilation, eating disorders, substance abuse, [and] impulsive risk-taking . . ." (p. 166). At least three of these–suicidality, eating disorders, and impulsive risk-taking–are often present in alcoholics' active drinking. And they frequently continue far into recovery. Although the links between these self-harming behaviors and the traumatic effects of homophobia are not always clear, there certainly has been a great amount of discussion about the amount and effects of substance abuse in the lesbian and gay communities. The most current studies do not support the assertion that "addiction rates are higher among lesbians and gay men, [but] some studies find that lesbians and gay men reported higher rates of AOD-related [alcohol and other drugs] problems" (Proceedings, 1992: p. 13). The contention is that many gay people drink alcoholically to try to soothe their feelings and to not care about the homophobia they constantly encounter and must deal with. Studies by McKirnan and Peterson (1989a & b) and Hall (1990a & b) support that discrimination because of sexual orientation is related to AOD-related problems. In addition, McKirnan and Peterson (1989a & b) found that "bar orientation" (how important the bar setting was to a person) was a very strong predictor of AOD-related problems reported by lesbians and gay men. Given the central social function of bars in many lesbian and gay communities, alcohol especially becomes readily available to those with a strong bar orientation. McKirnan and Peterson (1989a & b) also found that those lesbians and gay men least likely to report AOD-related problems are those who have a positive lesbian/gay identity.

Certainly the statistics about suicide are chillingly clear in indicating the traumatic effects of homophobia on young people. In his 1989 study, Gibson "concluded that lesbian and gay youth are two to three times more likely than their heterosexual counterparts to attempt suicide" (Cited by D'Augelli, 1994: pp. 16-17). In his 1991-1992 study of 200 lesbian and gay youth, D'Augelli (1994) produced even more terrible statistics:

> There was much evidence of suicidality. Only 40% said they had never thought about killing themselves. Many—42%—said they had made a past suicide attempt. (For comparison, high school suicide attempts rate estimates vary from 6% to 13%). (p. 18)

Herman (1992) also describes other forms of physiological harm resulting from trauma:

> The physiological changes suffered by chronically trauma-tized people are often extensive. People who have been subjected to repeated abuse in childhood may be prevented from developing normal sleep, eating, or endocrine cycles and may develop extensive somatic symptoms and abnormal pain perception. (p. 183)

There are striking parallels between these changes cited here and the changes observed in alcoholics. Both in their active addiction and in early recovery, alcoholics' sleep and eating patterns are often seriously disturbed and their somatic problems are indeed extensive. Although less is known about the physiological changes brought on by the trauma of homophobia, D'Augelli (1994) provides some insight into this matter:

> Coming out . . . at earlier ages, these [gay and lesbian youth] are at higher risk for harassment and violence than more closeted earlier generations. This victimization in turn affects their

mental health; and for some . . . the verbal taunts, threats, and punches may induce self-destructive impulses. (p. 18)

Furthermore, the following speculation seems well validated by the findings about other traumas: that fear–constant, on-going, un-relenting–fear of discovery, rejection, physical and emotional vio-lence take a tremendous toll on a person's psyche. It seems reason-able to assume that the effects of such fear, over time, would be traumatizing and would result in some of the same sequelae that other traumas produce such as disruptions in self-care, self-harming behaviors, and "a degree of physiological disturbance" (Herman, 1992: p. 187) continuing far into the process of recovery.

GENERAL CONSIDERATIONS

Taking into account the traumatizing effects of alcoholism and homophobia (even without regard to any other possible traumas), it is not hard to understand why it could be extremely difficult for an alcoholic lesbian or bisexual woman to develop a solid, integrated recovering self. Unfortunately, some or many of the traumatic se-quelae of both alcoholism and homophobia are the unavoidable consequences of being an alcoholic lesbian or bisexual woman.

Treating these women, therefore, is a difficult and complex task, a task made even more complex by such considerations as the woman's stage of recovery, especially in relation to relapse poten-tial; her stage of development of lesbian or bisexual identity; her family history; her history–if any–of physical, emotional and/or sexual abuse; the quality of her psychological defenses; and the strength of her support systems.

TREATMENT CONSIDERATIONS

The first, the foremost, and the most important consideration in treatment *always* is where a woman is in her alcohol/drug recovery process. This evaluation has far less to do with the number of years in recovery–although that issue is important–and far more to do with the stability of her life and the strength of her support net-works. If, for example, a lesbian or bisexual woman has over five years of recovery, but has had great difficulty holding jobs, has had numerous ruptured relationships, has "run through" three or four (or more) sponsors, and has few, if any, close friends, then her relapse potential may be rather high. Certainly, her profile would strongly caution against delving into past events which may have been traumatic and against focusing on issues other than those which would help her strengthen her support networks and achieve more stability in her work and personal relationships. Another ex-ample might be that of the lesbian or bisexual woman who has only three years of sobriety, but has a stable job, has a number of close friends, enjoys an active dating life, and has a good working rela-tionship with her sponsor. Her likelihood for relapse is low, so she is in a safer position to explore other areas such as possible childhood abuse or the development of her lesbian or bisexual identity, areas which might be problematic, difficult, or painful. One other exam-ple might be that of a woman who *has* relapsed because she felt overwhelmed by flashbacks of childhood sexual abuse. The thera-pist needs to help her focus on the tasks of early sobriety and especially help her to contain her flashbacks, rather than delve into them and thereby exacerbate her PTSD.

A second important consideration in evaluating and planning treatment is just where the woman is in the development of her sexual/affectional identity. For example, a woman may have been so traumatized by both external and internalized homophobia that she continues to be terrified of coming out to anybody or of attend-ing gay/lesbian AA meetings, even though she may have been in recovery for five or more years. Assisting her to explore both soci-ety's and her own homophobia and the traumatic sequelae of it rather than trying to get her to go to gay/lesbian AA would no doubt be the more helpful path. Another example of the stage of identity development might be the woman who is immersed in a long-term relationship, committed to her lesbian relationship, but not involved in any kind of community and thus isolated. She might well need help developing a wider support network of friends and AA peers. As Dillon (1993) points out, she probably also needs help with "the residual effects of hiddenness and duplicity on . . . [her] efforts to form a healthy, esteemed, integrated self" (p. 1).

A third consideration is that of family history. If her family is dysfunctional, especially if one or both parents have been or are active alcoholics, she will probably need much concrete help with the most basic tasks of self-care such as tending to personal hygiene, managing money, managing time, eating properly, getting enough sleep, planning her life. Since growing up in a dysfunctional family system creates problems such as these, therapists need to watch for such self-care deficits in many areas of a person's life far into her recovery. In addition, the history taker needs to explore possibilities of serious neglect and of physical, emotional, and/or sexual abuse. If evidence of these traumas is present, then the therapist must make decisions about when, how much, how intensely (if at all) to work on the neglect or abuse issues in relation especially to the client's recovery status.

Even if the lesbian recovering alcoholic comes from a relatively stable, functional family system, the history taking process must include questions about any possibilities of sexual abuse, employing, of course, a broad, inclusive definition of sexual abuse (both overt and covert forms of abuse). The questioner must listen closely and sensitively, evaluating the answers in light of the traumatic sequelae already known to exist because of the woman's status as a lesbian or bisexual woman who is recovering from alcoholism, and then make treatment decisions.

Another consideration for treatment planning and procedure is that of the strength and nature of the client's defenses. If the client tends to deny and minimize the need for a high degree of personal safety in her life (e.g., she doesn't exercise good judgment about walking alone in dangerous areas; she trusts people who end up harming or exploiting her), then the therapeutic work will need to focus on establishing safety rather than on investigating traumatic material. Another example might be the woman who is obsessive-compulsive and who engages in activities that are harmful to her such as compulsive sexual behavior, spending, overeating. Again, the primary therapeutic task is to help establish safety and to teach other ways to self-soothe. Another consideration is whether a person's defensive system can withstand such stresses as floods of memories or loss of sleep or psychosomatic problems. If the person is overwhelmed by affects and experiences, the therapeutic task would be first of all to teach how to contain feelings. Ultimately, the major evaluation must be about how rigid, how brittle, how flexible, how strong each person's defenses are. The therapeutic work must be adjusted accordingly.

One last issue must be considered–how strong, how extensive is a person's support system. If a woman has no close friends, has no supportive family (or instead has a dysfunctional, assaultive one), does not belong to a 12-step or other self-help program, then she is at risk for relapse and needs help establishing some kind of support network. She certainly is not in a safe position to do deep, complex, psychodynamic work at that point. The abuses she has suffered, whatever they may be, have isolated and disempowered her. For recovery, she needs support and connections that will empower her.

PRIMARY TREATMENT RESPONSIBILITIES

Of the many responsibilities involved in proper treatment, five stand out.

1. Above all else, Herman (1992) stresses, safety must be established and maintained. If a recovering alcoholic lesbian is threatened by homophobic forces–for example, if she will lose her job if her sexual orientation becomes known–she needs to be helped to protect herself and her identity and to feel all right about staying closeted. If an alcoholic bisexual woman with many years' recovery is severely depressed, she needs to receive specific treatment that will help alleviate the depression.

But safety also has to do with the character and training of the treating person. If the therapist knows about and accepts his/her limitations, that alone will offer some safety to the patient. But therapists who work with lesbians or bisexual women who are recovering alcoholics need to know about alcoholism, homophobia, and sexual abuse in order to provide the safest possible treatment. Such knowledge can help therapists focus on clients' alcoholism if there are relapse issues present; can help therapists balance between working on sexual abuse and other issues such as developing a positive sexual-affectional identity; and can help them support clients who are struggling with the dual stigmas of homophobia and alcoholism. If, however, the therapist is ignorant of the signs and symptoms of relapse, or does not know about dissociation, or is homophobic, even subtly so, then his/her recovering alcoholic lesbian or bisexual patients are not likely to be safe.

Herman (1992) talks about the issue of safety in working with childhood sexual abuse victims, an issue that has far-reaching implications. As she says,

> probably the second most common [therapeutic] error is premature or precipitate engagement in exploratory work, without sufficient attention to the tasks of establishing safety and securing a therapeutic alliance. (p. 172)

She then gives an example of a person in early recovery who would not go to AA and who was suddenly flooded with memories of abuse. The therapist, at the urging of the client, began doing intensive abuse work. As Herman (1992) points out, the therapist "failed to recognize that exploring traumatic memories in depth was likely to stimulate more intrusive symptoms of post-traumatic stress and therefore to jeopardize the patient's fragile sobriety" (p. 173). She goes on to note that thorough evaluation of the patient's current status is essential to ensuring safety and thereby protecting the patient. This caveat applies to *all* alcoholics in recovery, no matter what stage of recovery they may be in. Bean (1981) also stresses that safety must underly everything else.

2. As Herman (1992) notes, in survivors of chronic childhood abuse, "Self-care is almost always severely disrupted" (p. 166). Bean (1981), Mack (1981), and Khantzian (1981) also describe the disruption or lack of self-care stemming from the traumatic effects of alcoholism. And those who work with recovering alcoholic gay and lesbian clients (Finnegan & McNally, 1987; Kus, 1988; McNally, 1989) discuss the deficits in self-care that have developed in part as a result of responses to homophobia *and* alcoholism.

Thus, teaching self-care becomes a primary treatment responsibility. It is important to teach clients how to perform what are described as all the tasks of early sobriety. They are actually the tasks that a traumatized person does not know to *do* and does not know *how* to do. They may include such matters as dealing with obsessions to drink and/or drug, managing one's time, handling one's money, and protecting oneself (e.g., handling assaultive or intrusive others; taking proper self-defensive precautions).

In addition, therapy must help clients deal with whatever self-harming behaviors they may be engaging in–from eating disorders to self-mutilation to impulsive risk-taking. Since these behaviors serve to help people soothe their intolerable feelings, therapy needs to address and teach other ways to regulate feeling states.

3. Clients need to be helped to recognize, name, and express their feelings and to learn how to cope with those feelings. They need to learn how to regulate feeling states, how to contain feelings, how to safely express them. They also need to learn how to respond to others' feelings in ways appropriate to and supportive of their own well-being.

4. Another treatment responsibility is to encourage and assist clients to engage in mourning their losses which may range from a childhood lost to abuse to all the losses incurred in active alcoholism to the losses produced by homophobia (e.g., loss of status, loss of friends/family/job).

5. Primary also to effective treatment is the task of helping to de-shame and de-stigmatize the client. Shame and stigma are the results of abuse, whether it be sexual abuse, physical violence, alcoholism, or homophobia. The sufferer blames herself, "reasoning" that she must have been bad, that otherwise this evil would not have happened to her. If sexually abused, children are often told that they liked it, that they asked for it. If physically abused, the person is often blamed for "provoking" the perpetrator. If the person falls prey to alcoholism, she "brought it on herself," she "asked for it"; no matter how much public information is presented, many people still see alcoholism as "self-inflicted." If a person is attacked from without and within by homophobia, she must hear that she is "sick," "sinful," "perverted," "unnatural," "immoral," and/or "insane." To be attacked by any one of these, much less *all* of them, is to be subjected to powerful shaming forces. And to "own" any of these states of being is to take on a stigmatized identity.

Clients need to be able to work through the shame they experience from being traumatized. They need to transform their stigmatized identity into a positive one in order to heal. It is the task and the privilege of the therapist to accompany them and assist them on their healing journey.

ENDNOTES

1. This population includes many women who do not know what their sexual orientation is and whose search for such knowledge may take many years.
2. We define "long-term" as five or more years of continuous recovery.
3. The term "gay people" is to be understood as inclusive of bisexual women and men.

REFERENCES

Alvarez, W. (1994, March). *Sanctioned bias: Homophobia and its impact upon the therapeutic process.* Paper presented at the Meeting of the New York State Society for Clinical Social Work, Metropolitan Chapter, New York, NY.

Anderson, S.C., & Henderson, D.C. (1985). Working with lesbian alcoholics. *Social Work, 30*(6), 518-525.

Balint, M. (1964). *The doctor, his patient and the illness.* New York: International Universities Press.

Bean, M.H. (1981). Denial and the psychological complications of alcoholism. In M.H. Bean, E.J. Khantzian, J.E. Mack, G.E. Vaillant, & N.E. Zinberg (Eds.), *Dynamic approaches to the understanding and treatment of alcoholism* (pp. 55-96). New York: Free Press.

Courtois, C. (1988). *Healing the incest wound: Adult survivors in therapy.* W.W. Norton & Co.

D'Augelli, A.R. (1994, January). Attending to the needs of our youth: Focus on lesbian, gay and bisexual youth. *Division 44 Newsletter [American Psychological Association], 9*(3), 16-18.

Davies, J.M., & Frawley, M.G. (1994). *Treating the adult survivor of childhood sexual abuse: A psychoanalytic perspective.* New York: Basic Books.

Denzin, N. (1987). *The alcoholic self.* Beverly Hills: Sage.

Denzin, N. (1987). *The recovering alcoholic.* Beverly Hills: Sage.

Dillon, C. (1993). Developing self and voice in therapy with lesbians. *Developments: The Newsletter of the Center for Women's Development at HRI Hospital, 2*(3), 1,5.

EMT Group, Inc. (1992, October). *Proceedings: The research symposium on alcohol and other drug problem prevention among lesbians and gay men.* Sacramento, CA: California Department of Alcohol and Drug Problems.

Finnegan, D.G., & McNally, E.B. (1987). *Dual identities: Counseling chemically dependent gay men and lesbians.* Center City, MN: Hazelden.

Finnegan, D.G., & McNally, E.B. (1980). How to see (and help) the invisible lesbian alcoholic. Unpublished paper, presented at NADC, Washington, DC.

Finnegan, D.G., & McNally, E.B. (1990). Lesbian women. In R.C. Engs (Ed.), *Women: Alcohol and other drugs* (pp. 149-156). Dubuque, IA: Kendall/Hunt Publishing Co.

Finnegan, D.G., & McNally, E.B. (1989). The lonely journey: Lesbians and gay men who are co-dependent. In B. Carruth & W. Mendenhall (Eds.), *Co-dependency: Issues in treatment and recovery* (pp. 121-134). New York: The Haworth Press, Inc.

Hall, J.M. (1990a). Alcoholism in lesbians: Developmental, symbolic interactionist, and critical perspectives. *Health Care for Women International, 11*, 89-107.

Hall, J.M. (1990b). Alcoholism recovery in lesbian women: A theory in development. *Scholarly Inquiry for Nursing Practice: An International Journal, 4*(2), 109-125.

Herman, J.L. (1992). *Trauma and recovery: The aftermath of violence–from domestic abuse to political terror.* New York: Basic Books.

Kasl, C.D. (1993). *Many roads, one journey: Moving beyond the 12 steps.* New York: HarperCollins.

Khantzian, E. (1981). Some treatment implications of the ego and self disturbances in alcoholism. In M. Bean & N. Zinberg (Eds.), *Dynamic approaches to the understanding and treatment of alcoholism* (pp. 163-188). New York: The Free Press.

Krystal, H. (1988). *Integration & self-healing: Affect, trauma, alexithymia.* Hillsdale, NJ: Analytic Press.

Kurtz, E., & Ketcham, K. (1992). *The spirituality of imperfection: Modern wisdom from classic stories.* New York: Bantam.

Mack, J. (1981). Alcoholism, AA, and the governance of the self. In M. Bean & N. Zinberg (Eds.), *Dynamic approaches to the understanding and treatment of alcoholism* (pp. 128-162). New York: The Free Press.

McCann, I.L., & Pearlman, L. (1990). *Psychological trauma and the adult survivor: Theory, therapy, transformation.* New York: Brunner/Mazel.

McKirnan, D.J., & Peterson, P.L. (1989a). Alcohol and drug use among homosexual men and women: Epidemiology and population characteristics. *Addictive Behaviors, 14*, 545-553.

McKirnan, D.J., & Peterson, P.L. (1989b). Psychosocial and social factors in alcohol and drug abuse: An analysis of a homosexual community. *Addictive Behaviors, 14*, 555-563.

McNally, E.B. (1989). *Lesbian recovering alcoholics in Alcoholics Anonymous: A qualitative study of identity transformation.* Unpublished doctoral dissertation, New York University, New York.

Morales, E.S., & Graves, M.A. (1983). *Substance abuse: Patterns and barriers to treatment for gay men and lesbians.* San Francisco: Department of Public Health, Community Substance Abuse Services.

Nicoloff, L.K., & Stiglitz, E.A. (1987). Lesbian alcoholism: Etiology, treatment, and recovery. In Boston Lesbian Psychologies Collective (Eds.), *Lesbian psychologies: Explorations & challenges* (pp. 283-293). Urbana: University of Illinois Press.

Pellegrini, A. (1992). S(h)ifting the terms of hetero/sexism: Gender, power, homophobias. In W.J. Blumenfeld (Ed.), *Homophobia: How we all pay* (pp. 39-56). Boston: Beacon.

Pharr, S. (1988). *Homophobia: A weapon of sexism.* Little Rock: Chardon Press.

Rudy, D.R. (1989). *Becoming alcoholic: Alcoholics Anonymous and the reality of alcoholism.* Carbondale, IL: Southern Illinois University Press.

Ryan, W.P. (1991). Treatment issues with adult children of alcoholics. *Psychoanalytic Psychology, 8*(1), 69-82.

Shernoff, M. (Ed.). (1991). *Counseling chemically dependent people with HIV illness.* New York: The Haworth Press, Inc.

Shernoff, M. (1984). *Family therapy for lesbian and gay clients. Social Work, 29*(4), 393-396.

Shernoff, M., & Finnegan, D. (1991). Family treatment with chemically dependent gay men and lesbians. In E.B. Isaacson (Ed.), *Chemical dependency: Theoretical approaches and strategies working with individuals and families* (pp. 121-135). New York: The Haworth Press, Inc.

Silverstein, C. (1991). *Gays, lesbians, and their therapists: Studies in psychotherapy.* New York: W. W. Norton.

Stein, T.S., & Cohen, C.J. (Eds.). (1986). *Contemporary perspectives on psychotherapy with lesbians and gay men.* New York: Plenum Press.

Swallow, J. (Ed.). (1983). *Out from under: Sober dykes & our friends.* San Francisco: Spinsters, Ink.

van der Kolk, B.A. (1987). *Psychological trauma.* Washington, DC: American Psychiatric Press.

Weinstein, D.L. (Ed.). (1992). *Lesbians and gay men: Chemical dependency treatment issues.* New York: The Haworth Press, Inc.

Whitman-Walker Clinic. (Eds.). (1981). *The way back: The stories of gay and lesbian alcoholics.* Washington, DC: Whitman-Walker Clinic.

Woititz, J.G. (1983). *Adult children of alcoholics.* Deerfield Beach, FL: Health Communications, Inc.

Ziebold, T.O., & Mongeon, J.E. (Eds.). (1985). *Gay and sober: Directions for counseling and therapy.* New York: Harrington Park Press.

HIV, Women and Alcohol Recovery: Risks, Reality and Responses

J. D. Benson, MS, MFCC
Marcia Quackenbush, MS, MFCC
Diane K. Haas

SUMMARY. Both active and recovering alcoholics face genuine HIV-related risks. Additional risks exist for women alcoholics. Because of the serious nature of HIV disease, it is essential that recovery providers address HIV prevention in their work. Providers are encouraged to develop skills for discussing sexuality and HIV with women in recovery. Five principles are described, applicable to both individual and group work, which help establish a framework for discussions of sexuality and HIV in the context of recovery. Additionally, programs and providers are urged to direct attention to the issues of HIV positive women in recovery, including building skills in self-advocacy and assertiveness. *[Article copies available from The Haworth Document Delivery Service: 1-800-342-9678 E-mail address: getinfo@haworth.com.]*

In the early years of the HIV epidemic, alcohol recovery providers did not generally see AIDS as an issue of special relevance to

---

J. D. Benson, Marcia Quackenbush, and Diane K. Haas are affiliated with AIDS Health Project, University of California, San Francisco.

Portions of this article are adapted from M. Quackenbush, J. D. Benson, and J. Rinaldi, *Risk and recovery: AIDS, HIV and alcohol.* UC San Francisco: USSF AIDS Health Project, Box 0884, San Francisco, CA 94143, 1992.

[Haworth co-indexing entry note]: "HIV, Women and Alcohol Recovery: Risks, Reality and Responses." Benson, J. D., Marcia Quackenbush, and Diane K. Haas. Co-published simultaneously in *Journal of Chemical Dependency Treatment* (The Haworth Press, Inc.) Vol. 6, No. 1/2, 1996, pp. 109-127; and: *Chemical Dependency: Women at Risk* (ed: Brenda L. Underhill, and Dana G. Finnegan) The Haworth Press, Inc., 1996, pp. 109-127; and: *Chemical Dependency: Women at Risk* (ed: Brenda L. Underhill, and Dana G. Finnegan) Harrington Park Press, an imprint of The Haworth Press, Inc., 1996, pp. 109-127. Single or multiple copies of this article are available from The Haworth Document Delivery Service [1-800-342-9678, 9:00 a.m. - 5:00 p.m. (EST) E-mail address: getinfo@ haworth.com].

their work. It was gay men and injection drug users who were most immediately and deeply affected by AIDS, and their visibility in alcohol recovery programs was limited. Not until some years into the epidemic were two facts of particular importance to alcoholics widely understood: first, that HIV could be transmitted between any combination of people, whatever their gender or sexual orientation, if they engaged in unprotected sex or shared injection equipment; second, that the use of alcohol or other non-injection drugs was often linked with high rates of unsafe sexual behaviors or experimentation with injection drugs. Was it reasonable, providers wondered, to predict a high HIV risk for people in alcohol recovery?

Epidemiologic studies now confirm the legitimacy of these concerns. A number of studies have found surprisingly high rates of HIV infection among individuals in alcohol treatment programs, even in the absence of injection drug history or male-to-male sexual practices (Avins, Woods, Lindan et al., 1994; Mahler, Stebinger and Yi, in press). Further, the extensive practice of polydrug use has led providers to an understanding that substance use patterns may pose considerable direct HIV risk (e.g., through the sharing of needles), even in individuals who identify alcohol as their primary drug of choice. Providers working in the recovery field have responsibilities as a consequence of these findings and realizations: to stay well-informed about the HIV epidemic and its implications for participants; to develop a range of strategies and interventions that educate and inform participants about HIV and help them build personal skills for risk reduction; and to establish a sense of community understanding and support for individuals in recovery living with HIV.

The specific needs of women in recovery present a further challenge. It is not enough to share information about HIV-related risks with women in recovery. It is also necessary to cultivate an interrelated set of skills, capabilities and attitudes that allow women to evaluate such information in relation to their own behaviors; make choices about current and future behaviors based on that information; and have the skills in negotiation, assertiveness, and refusal strategies to stand by those choices. These are the actions of women with self-confidence (an ability to trust themselves and their assessments), self-esteem (belief in their own value), and self-efficacy (belief they can have an impact on their own lives).

Women in recovery face unique issues in relation to the HIV epidemic, including the limited attention paid to their risks and the more limited range of prevention interventions directed toward their situations and needs. While some resources address broader issues of HIV and recovery (Quackenbush, Benson and Rinaldi, 1992; Mukluscak-Cooper and Miller, 1991), little has been written about the specific concerns of women in recovery in relation to HIV.

In this article, our focus is specifically on women alcoholics in recovery. However, polydrug use is an extremely common practice among alcoholics, and the suggestions here will, for the most part, be generalizable to individuals who have used many different substances, and to those whose drug of choice is something other than alcohol.

HIV RISKS FOR ALCOHOLICS

A range of HIV risks face active and recovering alcoholics. Active users, especially when they are mildly inebriated, may become disinhibited and more impulsive. In some cases, this is associated with an increase in unsafe sexual behaviors. Studies investigating a specific causal effect between alcohol use and unsafe sex have reached mixed conclusions (Leigh and Stall, 1993), though in some instances alcohol use is clearly linked with unsafe sexual practices (Trocki and Leigh, 1991; McCusker, Westenhouse, Stoddard et al., 1990; Stall, Heurtin-Roberts, McKusick et al., 1990; Bagnall, Plant and Warwick, 1990). It is also possible that alcohol abuse serves as a marker for people who have risk-taking personalities generally, and that drinking and unsafe sexual practices are two distinct manifestations of that characteristic. Participants in alcohol recovery programs have reported high rates of unsafe sexual practices (Avins, Woods, Lindan et al., 1994).

Other risks are also evident. For example, individuals who experience blackouts may be unaware of behaviors practiced during these episodes, and have limited capability of either assessing risks accurately or making modifications in behavior. Laboratory studies have suggested a variety of possible biological effects that might increase susceptibility to HIV infection for drinkers, particularly if they engage in sexual activity during or soon after alcohol consumption (Bagasra, Kajdacsy and Lischner, 1989; Bagasra, Kajdacsy-Balla, Lischner and Pomerantz, 1993). Polydrug users, even if their drug of choice is alcohol, may try other substances, including heroin, cocaine or speed, all of which can be injected. When needles are shared in these circumstances, the risk of HIV transmission is increased.

Additionally, there are potential future risks for people who are currently in recovery and are not infected with HIV. Not all participants will succeed in a given effort to remain clean and sober, and those who relapse will be placed again in the higher cycle of risk facing the active alcoholic. And while most programs advise participants in early recovery to avoid new romantic or sexual relationships, many individuals have current partners, or will eventually have new sexual partners. These partners may be active users, or may come from the recovery community, with all its associated HIV risks.

RISKS FOR WOMEN

A number of factors complicate HIV risks for women alcoholics. Alcohol use is legal, culturally sanctioned, and in some ways more insidious than other drug use. Women are less likely than men to seek treatment, and are socialized to be "other" oriented–concerned with partner, children, or extended family more than with self. They are generally more likely to identify the source of problems as economic or social, and less likely to look at the effects of drinking behaviors in creating or exacerbating life problems. It is widely recognized that women trade sex for other drugs, but the practice of trading sex for alcohol also has a long history. These factors decrease the likelihood that women alcoholics will fully identify ways that patterns of drinking contribute to HIV risk behaviors.

The HIV-related risks for women are the same as those for anyone else: when the blood, semen or vaginal secretions of a person infected with HIV are taken into the body, a woman can become infected. However, the epidemiologic picture of women and HIV is unique and disturbing. Women are one of the fastest growing groups of individuals being infected with HIV. In the earliest years of the epidemic, women accounted for only 3% of AIDS cases in the United States. Today that percentage has risen to 12% (Centers for Disease Control and Prevention, 1993). These statistics are even more alarming in light of the fact that reported AIDS cases represent HIV infection trends that occurred five to ten years ago, because most people carry HIV asymptomatically for many years before receiving an AIDS diagnosis.

Avoiding HIV infection requires a kind of self-determination not all women have. Many women experience their sense of self-worth and value through an association with a husband or sexual partner. When a woman insists her partner abide by safer sex practices, the partner may threaten to leave the relationship, thus compromising the woman's sense of self, meaning and purpose. There are instances where women have been physically or sexually abused after requesting that their partners use condoms or other safer sex techniques. Even with a supportive partner, many women are not comfortable with the language or social techniques necessary to negotiate safer sexual practices. A woman who takes a lead in such interactions may also see herself, or fear being seen by partners or others, as challenging notions of gender role and "appropriate" female behavior.

These experiences are typically heightened for the chemically dependent woman. Problems of low self-esteem, poor social skills and lack of assertiveness are common. Self-doubt and lack of confidence color many social and sexual interactions. A secondary issue of co-dependency affects many chemically dependent women. Putting her own needs into the picture may present a greater challenge over time in a woman's ongoing recovery process than she faces in "staying away from that first drink." Concerns for risks to a partner often outweigh concerns for her own safety, even though women are more likely to be sexually infected by male partners than vice versa (Padian, Shiboski and Jewell, 1991). It may be difficult for her to consider the possibility that unsafe sexual practices are putting *her* at risk for HIV.

The sexual experiences of women in recovery are inextricably linked with their history and experience of drinking–many have never had sex without using alcohol or other substances. Because alcoholics tend to experience slowed emotional development while they are drinking, sexual feelings in sobriety bring up a range of responses more typically associated with adolescence. A woman in recovery well into her adult years may feel like a 13-year-old as she experiences feelings of attraction, confusion, fear, delight or emotional or physical numbing in relation to her sexuality.

These are far from ideal circumstances under which to face the intricacies of sexual relationships in the HIV era. Nevertheless, this is the reality that must be faced. A healthy sexual life is one desirable outcome for a woman in recovery. In achieving this, she must learn both the rewards of intimacy and the real concerns facing her in relation to HIV and other health risks. Learning how to make healthy decisions is a part of the recovery process that must be applied in the arena of sexual expression as in all aspects of living.

CHALLENGES FOR PROVIDERS

It is not only the participant in recovery who is challenged by the necessity of learning about appropriate sexual strategies in these times. Talking about sexuality with people in recovery can bring up conflicts for providers as well. Providers may find, for example, that discussing sexual practices with clients or participants contradicts professional training or recovery philosophy. They may believe that they lack adequate knowledge about sexuality to be able to discuss it. And some providers may fear that discussions about sex, especially during early recovery, give mixed messages to participants who should be focusing on sobriety, not on sexuality. It is essential that providers examine and address their own comfort in these areas as a necessary component of working with people on issues of sexuality and HIV risk reduction (Gray and House, 1991).

Discussions of sexuality with women present further complications. Society at large does not have a comfortable stance in relationship to women's sexuality, and frank discussion of women's sexual physiology, emotions, responses and appetites is often viewed with some suspicion. Both providers and female participants may feel a kind of embarrassment in discussing sexuality, as if there is something improper, inelegant or, more likely, shameful in this endeavor.

Presumptions of heterosexuality can also color such discussions. It is important to recognize that women of different sexual orientations participate in recovery. This may include women who self-identify in one group but engage in behaviors associated with another group—for example, a heterosexually identified woman may have sex with women, a lesbian-identified woman may have sex with men, and a bisexually-identified woman may have sex only with women, or only with men. Women will benefit most from interactions with providers who address sexuality issues from an informed, non-judgmental posture. Discussions of women's sexuality will be effective when providers and participants alike acknowledge the presence of women of all sexual orientations in the recovery community.

Recovery providers also need to consider their personal relationship to the HIV epidemic–looking at their own behaviors, past and present–before they can competently discuss these concerns with participants. Interesting questions may arise in this context. For example, can a provider who does not practice safer sex be effective in HIV prevention counseling with recovery participants? Will a provider who has never undergone HIV testing, and who is unfamiliar with the emotional and practical demands of the process, provide reasoned and informed support to a woman in early recovery who is considering the HIV antibody test? Does a provider who has never looked honestly at his or her own risks have the ability to assist a client in a forthright and honest assessment of her HIV risk history? There are not necessarily "correct" answers to these kinds of questions, but they do bear careful consideration.

Talking About Sexuality

If participants are going to learn about HIV prevention, providers are going to have to talk with them about sexuality. The HIV epidemic has changed the ways in which providers must approach sexuality with women in recovery. It is critical that people in early recovery be clearly informed about HIV-related risks and understand their own behavior in relation to these risks. This involves the sharing of facts as well as an exploration of deeper issues of sexual identity and motivation. Without this knowledge and understanding, there is little chance participants will successfully follow safer sex guidelines.

Talking about sexuality can be difficult for both provider and participant. There is a special vulnerability each experiences during discussions of such personal matters. The work, however, is likely to be easier and more effective if some general principles are kept in mind.

Each of us is a sexual being, and sexuality can be a positive aspect of self-identity and recovery. Many alcoholics have engaged in self-destructive behaviors involving sexuality, and many have been victimized sexually by family members, friends and strangers. They may have hurt others in sexual activities. The process of recovery often includes waves of memories or realizations about past sexual violence that can be very painful. For some people, it seems easier to deny or avoid sexual identity rather than come to terms with these past experiences.

Everyone is a sexual being, however, and sexual identity is an important part of who a person is. This does not mean that people must be sexually active, but it does mean that they can understand their behavior and who they are in a larger sense by understanding how they express their sexuality. Accepting the sexual self is an essential step in building self-esteem and self-acceptance.

Discussions of sexuality can help people in recovery develop healthier ways of thinking about sex and acting on sexual feelings. Most alcoholics in early recovery, and many in later recovery, think about sex, or put energy into *not* thinking about sex. Avoidance of sexual issues, or denial that they exist, interferes with the development of rigorous honesty and thorough acceptance of the nature of being human, as a woman grows in recovery. Providers can have discussions with participants about sex in sobriety that build understanding of appropriate social and sexual behaviors. For example, it will be a new experience for many to have sexual feelings, to acknowledge such feelings, and to choose consciously neither to act on them, nor to drink as a way to blunt or enhance them.

Discussions of sexuality and safer sex reinforce honesty and save lives. Providers may feel that discussions of sexuality unnecessarily raise difficult emotions for the newly sober. Some programs reinforce this attitude and discourage discussions of sexual topics. But people in recovery need support learning to talk honestly and directly about all of their experiences and concerns. Discussions about sex make it more possible for the alcoholic in sobriety to follow guidelines that will protect her from HIV infection. By offering participants the opportunity to understand their own sexuality and take steps to protect their well-being, providers demonstrate re-spect, caring, and confidence in the participant's ability to deal forthrightly with a sober lifestyle.

Discussions of sexuality and safer sex should be paired with clear messages about protecting sobriety and focusing on recovery. Alcoholism is a life-threatening disease. Maintaining sobriety saves lives. Sobriety is an essential focus in any program of recovery.

When providers encourage alcoholics in recovery to explore their own sexual issues and learn more about sex and safer sex, they must also emphasize the need to avoid situations that might lead to drink-ing. Open and informative discussions of sex and sobriety may actually help participants stay more focused on their sobriety be-cause they are being given an opportunity to understand, validate and process their own sexual issues. Behavioral guidelines recom-mending sexual abstinence in early recovery make more sense when offered as part of an open discussion about sexuality.

Providers are most effective when they are non-judgmental about sexual preferences and practices. It is important for providers to accept people in recovery as they are. By modeling such accep-tance, providers can help recovering alcoholics learn more about accepting and loving themselves. This means that providers must think carefully about when to "practice acceptance" and when to confront a participant about issues related to sexuality. Providers may have personal judgments about issues such as sexual orienta-tion; having more than one sexual partner; going to sex clubs, bars or socials to have sex; having sex for pleasure, without love or emotional attachment; using vibrators, dildoes or other sex toys; and having sex with casual acquaintances.

Nothing about these practices themselves conflicts with sobriety or a commitment to recovery. The alcoholic's attitudes and feelings about the activity are more pertinent than the provider's. When working with participants on sexual issues, providers are encour-aged to evaluate such situations carefully, build positive feelings about sexuality, maintain the participant's trust by avoiding judg-mental comments, and keep the focus on recovery.

In early recovery, a time in which participant coping skills are often limited, providers and participants alike may retreat from addressing HIV concerns. Is this a flight from rigorous honesty, or a reasonable approach to a "slippery" situation and a risk of relapse? This dilemma may best be weighed as other vital health risks would be. A person in recovery at risk for heart disease or high blood pressure would certainly be counseled on strategies to prevent further risk. Someone with symptoms of serious illness, such as diabetes, cancer or liver disease, would be referred for medical evaluation. HIV, because of the stigma attached to it and its association with sexuality and drug use, is often treated differently, but this is neither prudent nor appropriate considering the true level of risk facing the alcoholic in recovery.

Sexual topics span a spectrum from concrete and specific issues to deeper, personal concerns. As in all matters of such a personal nature, discussions of sexuality and sex should be handled sensitively, with attention to cultural differences such as ethnicity, religious orientation, sexual orientation, and gender. The values and beliefs participants carry from childhood about sex, its purpose and whether or not it was okay to talk about, play a powerful role in feelings, attitudes, beliefs and behaviors in the present.

Many women in recovery have little education about the mechanics of sexuality, and discussions of the sexual response cycle, sexual health, and safer sex strategies all fall into the realm of "concrete" items for discussion. Out of such discussions, deeper personal issues often emerge, including self-esteem, anxiety about past or potential future sexual relationships, and concerns about past HIV risk behaviors. Discussions of sexuality also offer considerable opportunity to explore larger recovery issues and help participants anticipate and respond to potential problems. For example, a participant might want to work on a personal inventory (AA's Fourth Step) focusing on sexual history, or think about the step she is currently working and what that step suggests about sexual issues or concerns.

As individuals stop using alcohol or other drugs to mask feelings or experiences, they often experience a powerful flooding of memories. These may include incest or sexual abuse, rape, or other forms of sexual violence. Old experiences that seemed resolved suddenly arise again, bringing new memories of terrible pain or fear. Details of past experiences emerge with greater accuracy and intrusiveness. There is controversy about when during an individual's recovery such powerful issues should be addressed in depth. Does the risk of relapse increase by focusing on such difficult issues early in recovery? Or is it a greater risk to collude in a participant's denial and avoidance of such matters?

These situations can be evaluated on a case-by-case basis, with participants taking an active role in deciding the course of the work. For some, it may involve deep and immediate attention to the memories; for others a simple acknowledgement, shared with another person, that a particular event happened; for still others, an agreement to set aside in-depth work on the issue while focusing on building strength in a recovery program.

STRATEGIES AND INTERVENTIONS

No single approach to HIV education and skills-building for risk reduction will be appropriate for all women. And while many of the suggestions that follow are applicable to men in recovery as well, women do tend to respond enthusiastically to group interventions for sharing of knowledge and experience, developing skills, and building self-esteem and peer relationships. In one study, women in alcohol treatment were significantly more interested than men in "extensive and continuous care," including participation in AA, along with group, marital or individual counseling (Murphy and Hoffman, 1993).

Most recovery programs have regularly scheduled group sessions. Providers can integrate sexuality and health issues into these sessions as they might parenting skills or job search skills, making the discussions part of the program, not special or exceptional. The groups might address the concrete issues of sexual health, sexual function and HIV risk reduction, then build on the broader issues of how these topics affect attitudes, feelings and recovery in general. Through such approaches, HIV education and training will become more easily accepted by providers and participants alike.

Participants will also benefit from active learning opportunities. Role plays and interactive dramatic exercises can help women build assertiveness, develop refusal skills, and experience the process of decision-making and follow-through in "practice sessions" before facing similar challenges in real life. These skills translate across many topic areas, so it is not necessary to focus every activity on HIV risk reduction specifically. A range of other issues of immediate concern to many women in recovery can also be addressed in such groups–for example, seeing a medical provider and being an assertive consumer; negotiating through conflicts with roommates, partners or children; or asking for a job application at a local business.

Groups can also explore gender expectations and sex role issues, especially relations between women and men. These might include experiences in romantic or sexual relationships between men and women, as well as in other non-sexual interactions. For comparison, participants can also consider their expectations and personal feelings in same-gender groups, or in one-to-one relationships with same-sex friends or, where applicable, same-sex lovers.

Discussions of sex role expectations or HIV risks may also lead naturally into discussions of homophobia. It is helpful for participants to explore feelings and attitudes about sexual orientation. In many cases, people are less willing to look realistically at their own risks for HIV if they feel, in doing so, they are likely to be linked with homosexuality. Additionally, lesbians, gay men and bisexuals in recovery may feel they are not fully accepted by others. Frank and forthright discussions of homophobia can help people learn more about accepting differences and diversity, and create a more supportive and effective recovery community.

These kinds of interventions can be planned in mixed-gender groups. However, because many women in recovery have experienced sexual exploitation by men, feelings of trust and connectedness may develop more naturally in same-gender groups with a woman facilitator. It is essential for women to have positive women role models in their recovery, and in many cases this kind of sensitive exploration of sexuality and health will be most effective in women-only groups.

It may also be necessary to engage in special outreach, or set up particular and focused one-time or ongoing groups, to establish safety for some women participants. For example, it may be too great an obstacle to a group of newly sober women to have an open discussion about sex with a male discussion leader or male co-participants in their group. It may be unrealistic to expect that women who have had sex with women, regardless of their self-identified sexual orientation, will feel safe openly discussing their sexual behaviors with anyone unless acceptance and trust have been previously established.

Different kinds of interventions can be planned for women at different phases in recovery. For example, in the earliest months of recovery, attention must be given to a woman's risk of relapse. Careful evaluation of her responses to group and one-to-one discussions of HIV risks and related issues is a necessary component of this process, for both provider and participant. Providers should aim to develop baseline skills for survival (assertiveness, self-esteem, refusal strategies), and the primary focus throughout should be on the day-to-day process of building strength in recovery.

Some researchers have identified an important period of change in attitudes about sobriety at 12 to 18 months of recovery (Murphy and Hoffman, 1993). There is a shift from an identity as a "deprived user" to that of a "determined abstainer." In this period, discussions of sexual health and HIV risks can highlight changes in self-identity and the participant's relationship to drinking. If such change is possible in relation to drinking, it is certainly possible in any number of other personal arenas, including sexual behavior and the ability to make self-care and protection a priority.

Talking and thinking about HIV can actually help participants explore recovery issues at a specific, concrete level as well as in broader life terms. In the concrete realm, providers can help women evaluate past and present risks, and assess needs for behavior change. In the broader mix of life and recovery, providers can encourage discussions of change, progress, empowerment and serenity in relation to HIV concerns and considerations. Providers should manage such discussions with consideration and detachment. It is important, for example, that providers understand the difference between assessing HIV risk and, in 12-Step language, doing someone else's personal inventory.

The HIV-Positive Woman in Recovery

Some women will come into recovery knowing they have HIV, and others will test and be told they have HIV after beginning their recovery program. In either case, concerns about safety, confidentiality and support are likely to arise for the women affected. For their well-being, and that of the recovery community at large, it is essential that programs and providers have a foundation in place to respond to their needs.

There are people who continue to be afraid of "catching" HIV infection by being close to or touching people with HIV disease. There are others who are judgmental about people with HIV, believing they must have done something wrong to get it. And there are people who discount individuals with HIV disease, believing such people will die soon and do not need attention or service.

People with these beliefs can be found in the recovery community as both participants and providers. If they do not have an opportunity to educate themselves about HIV, they may never have the chance to develop opinions based on truth rather than conjecture. People with HIV will continue to suffer because of these misunderstandings and prejudices, and a poor environment for sobriety may result for all.

Providers can educate participants about HIV in a manner that establishes and maintains emotional safety for HIV-infected people. For example, new participants coming into programs should be educated about HIV transmission. This will include strategies to avoid infection, as well as clear information that HIV is not casually transmitted.

It is not generally useful for recovery providers to conceive of HIV infection as a fatal disease. Like alcoholism, HIV is a life-threatening, chronic, progressive disease. Treatments are available that can prolong health and well-being, and increase life span. Many people with HIV disease will live in good health for a decade or more, and as treatments improve, may live without related symptoms even longer.

Some women will learn they have HIV infection early in recovery. One of the first concerns of a woman who learns she has HIV is the possibility that children or a current sexual partner might also be infected. Questions about who should or should not be told about her HIV status are closely related to these concerns. Providers can guide a participant to make a thoughtful evaluation of who needs to know, including individuals at personal risk (present or past sexual or needle-sharing partners), as well as who she would like to tell to gain support. This evaluation can include ways the participant can best communicate this information to the selected individuals.

It is important that the woman exercises ultimate control in the matter of who to tell, when and how. Providers can assist with accurate information, and non-judgmental counseling. Telling others that one is HIV positive has significant health implications because in the hands of some people it can adversely affect emotional support and physical safety. Women may face a range of genuine obstacles to disclosure, especially to sexual or needle-sharing partners (including physical violence). Many county health departments have confidential or anonymous partner notification programs, and may be able to help the participant in this regard.

Women with HIV disease need to learn self-advocacy skills to deal successfully with the medical treatment system. They need to understand, for example, how to locate and utilize medical services, how to evaluate a physician's treatment recommendations, and where to go to learn about health or disability benefits. Because the physical manifestations of HIV are often different in women, and may involve a number of gynecologic complications, a woman must evaluate not only the physician's knowledge of HIV generally, but his or her familiarity with the specific medical issues of women with HIV.

Many of these steps will be difficult for a woman in early recovery. They require more than information. They require assertiveness, persistence, and self-assurance. Providers may need to help participants develop these skills. This can include helping people see what options are available to them, helping them work out action plans for the options they choose, and modeling ways to deal with service providers. It is important that participants make their own choices about issues of personal health and illness.

Providers can also maintain a good, up-to-date list of HIV-related referrals and resources. A number of newsletters for women with HIV are currently available, and names, addresses and telephone numbers for these kinds of resources should be offered to the woman with HIV.[1] HIV providers who are familiar with both HIV services and recovery issues should be identified. Whenever possible, publicly identified HIV-positive staff, educators, community workers, or other sources of support should be made available to women with HIV. Because women experience HIV in even greater isolation than most men, linking up women with HIV for one-to-one "buddy" relationships or for group support can be of immense value. Specific groups for women with HIV in recovery establish a positive environment for expressing concerns, gaining information, and sharing mutual support.

Providers and participants alike need to be reminded of the value of anonymity and confidentiality. Some individuals with HIV choose to be public about their situations, while others prefer to maintain privacy. Information shared in support groups with confidentiality ground rules, or in 12-Step meetings, should not be passed on to others. Unfortunately, there have been instances where members of the recovery community have had their anonymity or confidentiality violated in this regard. Even where the transgression is well meaning–someone expressing concern for the health of a participant heard to have HIV, for example–the breech of anonymity or confidentiality can be damaging. In situations where ignorance, homophobia and insensitivity also play a role, the results can be disastrous (Kus and Carpenter, 1991).

Grief and Loss: HIV and Alcohol

Discussions of HIV may also bring up feelings of grief and loss, for provider and participant alike. It is natural, in the course of life, that everyone experiences losses of different types. People in recovery, especially early in recovery, share the loss of their "good friend" alcohol and all of the social interactions that accompanied its use.

As HIV-related issues are discussed in more depth, other losses may be acknowledged: the loss of sexual freedom in the HIV era, the loss of friends or family to illnesses (cancer, liver disease, HIV), the loss of custody of children, the absence of support for residential recovery programs for women and their children. Part of the recovery process is learning to "take life on life's terms." Participants must learn to cope with the changes and losses that come along in the normal course of experience.

Providers can also address loss in group and one-to-one settings. In the same way participants can learn about recovery and identity generally by looking at issues of sexuality specifically, explorations of grief and loss can also reflect on the larger process of recovery. Participants need to develop a range of skills for coping with uncomfortable feelings without resorting to alcohol, and discussions of grief and loss can be helpful in this regard.

CONCLUSION

Providers who bring increased sensitivity and awareness to the issue of HIV and women in recovery help not only with HIV prevention specifically, but with other issues relevant to success of long-term sobriety and the well-being of the recovery community. It is important that providers guard against the feeling that these suggestions are too much to do, too difficult to understand, or too problematic to implement. For participants, self-assessment of HIV risk, facilitated by a knowledgeable provider, can be an important task in the overall process of healing. This process need not direct participants into "slippery territory," but can be framed in light of the health risks posed by HIV and other sexually or needle sharing transmitted disease.

HIV disease is in the alcohol recovery community today and is affecting women in that community. Providers can take part in the effort to respond by developing the knowledge and clinical skill necessary to help clients and program participants build effective personal strategies to avoid HIV. The complexity of alcohol recovery underscores the need for providers to understand and work with the larger contextual issues surrounding risk for HIV disease and addiction, two life threatening illnesses which are all too often linked in both the using and recovering communities of women.

NOTE

1. Four currently available newsletters are:

Women Being Alive
A newsletter written by and for women infected or affected by HIV/AIDS, in English and Spanish; 3626 Sunset Boulevard, Los Angeles, California 90026. (213) 667-3262.

WORLD

Women Organized to Respond to Life-threatening Diseases. A newsletter by, for and about women facing HIV disease, in English and Spanish, quarterly. P.O. Box 11535, Oakland, California 94611. (510) 601-9746.

The Positive Woman

National newsletter by, for and about women with HIV. P.O. Box 34372, Washington, D.C., 20043-4372. (202) 898-0372.

Positively Aware

The monthly journal of Test Positive Aware Network. TPA Network, 1340 W. Irving Park, Box 259, Chicago, Illinois 60613. (312) 404-TPAN.

CITATIONS

Avins AL, Woods WJ, Lindan CP, Hudes ES, Clark W, Hulley S, 1994. HIV infection and risk behaviors among heterosexuals in alcohol treatment programs. JAMA 271:515-518.

Bagasra O, Kajdacsy BA, Lischner HW, 1989. Effects of alcohol ingestion on in vitro susceptibility of peripheral blood mononuclear cells to infection with HIV and of selected T-cell functions. Alcoholism: Clinical and Experimental Research 13:636-643.

Bagasra O, Kajdacsy-Balla A, Lischner HW, Pomerantz RJ, 1993. Alcohol intake increases human immunodeficiency virus type 1 replication in human peripheral mononuclear cells. Journal of Infectious Diseases 167:789-797.

Bagnall G, Plant M, Warwick W, 1990. Alcohol, drugs and AIDS-related risks: results from a prospective study. AIDS Care 2:309-317.

Centers for Disease Control and Prevention, 1993. HIV/AIDS Surveillance Report 5:11.

Gray LA, House RM, 1991. Counseling the sexually active client in the 1990s: a format for preparing mental health counselors. Journal of Mental Health Counseling 13:291-304.

Kus RJ, Carpenter MA, 1991. Lance: a gay recovering alcoholic misdiagnosed as HIV-positive. Archives of Psychiatric Nursing 5:307-312.

Leigh BC, Stall RC, 1993. Substance use and risky sexual behavior for exposure to HIV: issues in methodology, interpretation and prevention. American Psychologist 48:1035-1045.

Mahler J, Stebinger A, Yi D et al. Reliability of admission history in predicting HIV infection among alcoholic inpatients. Am J Addict. In press. Cited in Avins, AL et al. 1994. HIV infection and risk behaviors among heterosexuals in alcohol treatment programs. JAMA 271:515-518.

McCusker J, Westenhouse J, Stoddard AM, Zapka JG, Zorn MW, Mayer KH, 1990. Use of drugs and alcohol by homosexually active men in relation to sexual practices. Journal of Acquired Immune Deficiency Syndrome 3:729-736.

Mikluscak-Cooper C, Miller EE, 1991. Living in hope: a 12-step approach for persons at risk or infected with HIV. Berkeley CA: Celestial Arts.

Murphy SA, Hoffman AL, 1993. An empirical description of phases of maintenance following treatment for alcohol dependence. Journal of Substance Abuse 5:131-143.

Padian NS, Shiboski SC, Jewell NP, 1991. Female-to-male transmission of Human Immunodeficiency Virus. JAMA 266:1664-1667.

Quackenbush M, Benson JD, Rinaldi J, 1992. Risk and recovery: AIDS, HIV and alcohol. San Francisco: UCSF AIDS Health Project.

Stall R, Heurtin-Roberts S, McKusick L, Hoff C, Lang S, 1990. Sexual risk for HIV transmission among singles-bar patrons in San Francisco. Medical Anthropology Quarterly 4:115-128.

Trocki K, Leigh B, 1991. Alcohol consumption and unsafe sex: a comparison of heterosexuals and homosexual men. Journal of Acquired Immune Deficiency Syndrome 4:981-986.

Women's Marijuana Problems:
An Overview with Implications
for Outreach, Intervention, Treatment,
and Research

Susan Chacín, BA

SUMMARY. Individual, cultural, professional, and gender-related factors converge to increase the denial of women's marijuana problems. Recent epidemiological information on marijuana use shows that marijuana is a significant problem for women of various ethnic groups, pregnant women, young adults and workers. Women's marijuana-related problems affect their health, safety, domestic relations, motherhood, and work. Outdated addiction theories, diagnostic tools, and insufficient research aggravate the difficulty of treating marijuana addiction. Current research and addiction theory show that marijuana should be classified with all other addictive drugs. Recommendations and resources are provided for marijuana-specific public outreach,

Susan Chacín is Executive Director of the Alcoholism Center for Women, a prevention and recovery program serving high-risk women with special outreach to lesbians. She has worked in the field of alcohol and other drug problems since 1980. As a planner for the Los Angeles County Alcohol and Drug Program Administration, she helped to identify unmet needs and organize community groups advocating for increased and improved services to women, lesbians, and gay men. In 1989, she left civil service to become Deputy Director of a community-based, social model recovery program.

Address correspondence to: Susan Chacín, ACW, 1147 South Alvarado Street, Los Angeles, CA 90006. E-mail address: CTET24A@Prodigy.com

[Haworth co-indexing entry note]: "Women's Marijuana Problems: An Overview with Implications for Outreach, Intervention, Treatment, and Research." Chacín, Susan. Co-published simultaneously in *Journal of Chemical Dependency Treatment* (The Haworth Press, Inc.) Vol. 6, No. 1/2, 1996, pp. 129-167; and: *Chemical Dependency: Women at Risk* (ed: Brenda L. Underhill, and Dana G. Finnegan) The Haworth Press, Inc., 1996, pp. 129-167; and: *Chemical Dependency: Women at Risk* (ed: Brenda L. Underhill, and Dana G. Finnegan) Harrington Park Press, an imprint of The Haworth Press, Inc., 1996, pp. 129-167. Single or multiple copies of this article are available from The Haworth Document Delivery Service [1-800-342-9678, 9:00 a.m. - 5:00 p.m. (EST) E-mail address: getinfo@haworth.com].

intervention, treatment and research. *[Article copies available from The Haworth Document Delivery Service: 1-800-342-9678. E-mail address: getinfo@haworth.com]*

BACKGROUND

Women's problems with marijuana are largely unexplored in the literature on drug addiction and treatment. It has only recently been recognized that women have unique chemical dependency issues, and marijuana problems are rarely discussed even for the general population.

This article will present what is known about marijuana problems among women and make suggestions for professionals in the areas of outreach, intervention, treatment, and research. Because so little is written about marijuana addiction in any population, basic information about marijuana addiction is also provided.

DENIAL OF WOMEN'S MARIJUANA PROBLEMS

Professionals in the field of addiction and recovery deal with denial all the time. However, denial of women's marijuana problems is very powerful. It is cumulative, deriving from several sources, and it acquires unique characteristics based on these origins. In broad terms, the denial of women's marijuana problems can be traced to four principal causes:

1. People with alcohol and other drug problems generally deny that they may be addicted, so much so that individual denial is sometimes considered a symptom of addiction.
2. With marijuana, individual denial is compounded by strong cultural messages which claim that marijuana is harmless or poses a very low risk of "psychological dependency."
3. The erroneous cultural beliefs which affect the general population are also found in the medical, mental health, social work, and chemical dependency fields. Professional denial in turn leads to the public receiving erroneous and misleading "official" information, to a lack of research on marijua-

na problems and their treatment, and to misguided responses to marijuana problems when presented in professional
practice.
4. Society's general denial of women's drug problems as compared
to men's makes it particularly difficult for a woman or those
around her to admit that she is an addict.

Denial of Marijuana Problems

Marijuana is the subject of more mixed messages than any other
drug in our society. Although marijuana is illegal in most areas,
penalties vary widely. Calls for legalization or decriminalization of
marijuana have been persistent for decades. Publicity about limited
medical usefulness of marijuana has given many the impression that
it is completely safe and even beneficial.

Our society's ambivalence about marijuana has a history of at
least thirty years. It is rooted in the transformations which began in
the 1960s social movements for civil rights, against the war in
Vietnam, for women's liberation, and for lesbian and gay rights.
Along with rock and roll music and the sexual revolution, it has
played a key role in the development of a new youth counter-culture. In 1968, Allen and West noted that:

> The role of marihuana and LSD is crucial in the hippie rebel-
> lion. . . . The future of the hippies and their rebellion depends
> in part upon the further evolution of society's reaction to them
> but also, and perhaps most importantly, upon the long-term
> effects of drugs chronically employed as the materia medica of
> a flight from aggression and violence. (p. 120)

The feature movie *Nine to Five* is a period example of romanti-
cized marijuana use as an avenue toward women's liberation. Lily
Tomlin, Jane Fonda, and Dolly Parton play exploited and harassed
office workers. After smoking a marijuana cigarette, they fantasize
how to get even with their sneaky, sexist, lying, male chauvinist pig
of a boss. Our heroines unexpectedly have a chance to act out their
pipe dreams and magically solve a wide array of office injustices
along the way. Their marijuana-inspired exploits contrast with the
stupor of a chronic alcoholic woman in the typing pool, but she

even gets sober thanks to her new feminist environment (Gilbert, 1980).

Counterproductive Prevention Efforts

Ironically, several efforts to publicize marijuana's risks have played into our culture's denial that marijuana is a problem. The 1936 film *Reefer Madness* (Gasnier) has become a cult classic by proving that warnings about marijuana's dangers have sometimes been exaggerated, simplistic, or aimed at the wrong population. Neither were the "Just Say No" and "War on Drugs" campaigns of the Reagan and Bush administrations likely to attract rebellious youth or chronic marijuana users.

The anti-drug parents' movement has had a significant impact on adolescent drug use in some areas. It grew out of local activist groups which coalesced in the Federation of Parents for Drug-Free Youth, now renamed the National Family Partnership. While these organizations have had some success in overcoming local communities' denial concerning marijuana, their approach has been problematic for other reasons.

One unintended consequence of the focus on adolescent use by these groups and by many researchers has been to create a new myth that marijuana is only a risk for adolescents. Another expression of this misconception is the emphasis on marijuana as a "gateway" drug, leading to the drugs which are better recognized as causing addiction. This can be misinterpreted to mean that marijuana itself is only a problem insofar as it increases a user's risk of progressing to "hard drugs."

The parental focus of many community prevention efforts has also had mixed consequences. While empowering parents and overcoming their denial of their children's problems, it may also have reinforced the rebellious attitudes of young people and adults who use marijuana to break away from mainstream values and norms. Use of marijuana can serve as a badge of independence from conservative values.

Denial of Women's Marijuana Problems

"Denial or disgust are the most common responses to female addiction" (Vandor, Juliana, & Leone, 1991, p. 155).

Our culture has highly polarized attitudes toward women, sometimes described as the dichotomy of the Madonna or the whore. Drugs, particularly when consumed by women, have a connotation of promoting active sexuality. Good women are not addicts, and addicts are not good women.

When a good woman identifies herself as having a drug or alcohol problem, people who care about her often have trouble accepting it. This denial can become a barrier to her recovery. Beckman and Amaro (1984) found that 23 percent of women entering treatment for alcoholism reported opposition from family and friends whereas only 2 percent of men faced any opposition. The one person who opposed a man's beginning recovery was a drinking companion.

Mary Docter, the Olympic speed skater, provided a striking example of a young woman's marijuana problems and family denial in an interview she gave in 1990.

> Up until last fall, 1990, I was buying marijuana by the half-ounce and smoking that morning, noon or night until it was all gone. I was smoking before class, after class, before I studied, after I studied, before I trained, after I trained. It was a serious addiction. It was something I needed and I thought I enjoyed it.

A college friend helped Docter find recovery, but her parents were not convinced:

> When I did tell them about my addiction, they said 'That's bull. . . .' My mother told me I wasn't an alcoholic. My dad said I shouldn't have told my classmate. They thought it was my own fault. They were denying it as well. I can understand that. Your parents want to think they have a healthy, happy family. (Harvey, 1990, pp. C1-2)

Docter's example points out an important unintended consequence of denial. If a person is not addicted, then she is to blame for her problems. In this way, ironically, denial can actually increase shame and guilt. In the absence of an understanding of addiction, the user is fully responsible for her lack of control.

EPIDEMIOLOGY

How prevalent are women's marijuana problems? Marijuana is the most widely used illicit drug in the United States today. Although women use marijuana at rates lower than men, the numbers of female users are still large. Marijuana represents a significant chemical dependency problem for women.

The Substance Abuse and Mental Health Services Administration (SAMHSA)(1993) estimated that in 1992 approximately 30 million women had ever used marijuana. Although almost as many women as men have tried marijuana, the gap between men's and women's use is larger for more frequent use. Estimated use patterns within the year prior to the study show that 1,683,000 women were using marijuana at least weekly compared to 3,485,000 male weekly users. It is interesting to note that across the three population groups for which data is presented separately, the rates of men's use at weekly or higher levels are consistently about two percentage points higher than women's. Detailed information from this study on marijuana use by ethnic and gender groups appears in Table 1.

Rates of Marijuana Use Among Various Ethnic and Cultural Groups

The SAMHSA study and other sources provide some information on differences in marijuana use by various ethnic and cultural groups of women.

African American Women

African American[1] women are using marijuana at higher rates than any other group of women. A pattern of weekly use over the past year was reported by 2.3 percent of African American women as compared to 1.5 percent of European American women and 1.4 percent of Latinas. African American women also showed the highest rate of marijuana use during pregnancy of any group in a perinatal study of women in California (Vega et al., 1993).

European American Women

European American women constitute the largest number of women using marijuana. Although their rates of use are slightly

TABLE 1. Number and Percent of Population Using Marijuana in the U.S. by Ethnicity and Gender – 1992

Population Group	Ever Used	Used Last Month	Used at Least Weekly for Last Year
Total Population:	67,525,000 32.8	8,950,000 4.4	5,168,000 2.5
Women	29,994,000 28.0	3,111,000 2.9	1,683,000 1.6
Men	37,531,000 38.0	5,839,000 5.9	3,485,000 3.5
African Americans:	7,358,000 31.1	1,227,000 5.2	749,000 32
Women	3,318,000 25.7	515,000 4.0	292,000 2.3
Men	4,040,000 37.6	712,000 6.6	457,000 4.3
European Americans:	54,243,000 34.2	6,929,000 4.4	3,901,000 2.5
Women	24,337,000 29.7	2,322,000 2.8	1,213,000 1.5
Men	29,906,000 39.1	4,607,000 6.0	2,688,000 3.5
Latinos:	4,364,000 25.9	632,000 3.7	418,000 2.5
Women	1,575,000 18.6	216,000 2.5	117,000 1.4
Men	2,789,000 33.3	416,000 5.0	300,000 3.6

National Household Survey on Drug Abuse: Population Estimates, 1992. Substance Abuse and Mental Health Services Administration, U.S. Department of Health and Human Services, Public Health Service, 1993. Data from tables 3-A - 3-D and 20-A - 20-D, pp. 25-27 and 109-111.[1]

lower than African American women, their numbers in the population are larger. European American use is high in the adolescent years and persists into the mid-thirties. Prenatal use of marijuana by white women was also found to be far higher than any other group except African Americans in the California perinatal study.

Latinas

Latinas have the lowest rates of marijuana use of any group summarized in the SAMHSA survey. Analysis of information collected between 1982 and 1984 suggests that within the Latina population, Puerto Rican women may use marijuana at the highest rate, followed by Mexican American women. Cuban American women showed the lowest rates of use (National Clearinghouse for Alcohol and Drug Information, 1989).

Information from the California perinatal survey, California, shows that U.S.-born Latinas' patterns of any illicit drug use are higher and closer to the European American population than foreign-born Latinas' rates.

Asian and Pacific Islander Women

Separate information for Asian and Pacific Islander population is not tallied in the SAMHSA survey. Asian and Pacific Islander women showed the lowest rates for marijuana use in the California perinatal study, but in the same survey, like U.S.-born Latinas, U.S.-born Asian women displayed increased rates of illicit drug use compared to foreign born women (Vega et al., 1993).

Native American Women

Again, the SAMHSA survey does not summarize drug use by Native Americans and neither does the California perinatal study. Anecdotal information suggests that Native American women's use of marijuana is increasing (Roth, 1991). An analysis of combined marijuana and alcohol use based on a 1982 survey found that four percent of Native women had used alcohol and marijuana in the past month compared to five percent of White and Black women (Norton & Colliver, 1988).

Lesbians and Bisexual Women

Lesbians and bisexual women are experiencing marijuana problems at extremely elevated rates.

The Trilogy study of lesbian and gay alcohol and other drug use around two cities in Kentucky found that 36.1 percent of lesbians had used marijuana in the past year compared to 8.2 percent of women in the 1988 National Household Survey of Drug Abuse. Higher rates of lesbian marijuana use were most pronounced in older cohorts. Whereas 18-25 year-old lesbians' rates of use in the past year were double that of the National Household survey, 26-34 year-olds used marijuana at four times the rate of the general population, and respondents over 35 used it at eight times the national average for women. The study found that 20.6 percent of lesbians had smoked marijuana in the past month (Skinner & Otis, 1992), a rate almost 10 times that of women in the 1992 National Household Survey (Substance Abuse and Mental Health Administration, 1993).

Another study of gay men and lesbians in Chicago found that frequent marijuana use was twice as common for lesbians 26-34 years of age as for the general population, and 30 times as common at age 35 and above (McKirnan & Peterson, 1992).

Ethnic Use by Age Groups

Both Latino and European American adolescents ages 12 to 17 use marijuana at rates higher than African American adolescents, 3.2 percent and 2.1 percent compared to 1.9 percent respectively. European American adults 26 to 34 years of age also show the highest weekly use rate for their age range.

Upswing in Use by School Age Youth

Recent school-year surveys of student use of marijuana have shown an upswing in use by adolescents, reversing a downward trend since 1978 ("Increased Use," 1993). An increased trend of adolescent marijuana use has also been evident in youth culture with the popularity of the rap group Cypress Hill and 1970s nostalgia movies such as "Dazed and Confused" (Jacks, 1993) and "The

Stoned Age" (Moritz & Heyman, 1993). Adolescent marijuana use has historically persisted into adulthood, with 50 percent of the daily smokers in the class of 1975 reporting continued daily use four years later (Kandel, 1992).

A phenomenon which has not been studied adequately is that many of today's adolescents are growing up in households where marijuana is or has been commonly used. High school seniors in the peak year of use, 1978, are about 35 years old in 1995, and any children they had at age 20 would be 15. This phenomenon may in part explain the tendency of attitudes toward drugs to take pendulum swings. Thus, many of today's parents' tolerant or even positive attitudes toward marijuana are based on their socialization during years when marijuana use was very frequent. These attitudes, combined with some parents' role modeling use and even addiction to the drug, make it probable that the trend toward increased marijuana use will continue.

WOMEN'S MARIJUANA PROBLEMS

Belying marijuana's reputation for safety, 20 percent of people who have ever tried marijuana have experienced symptoms of abuse or dependence. Kandel asserts that once having tried an illicit drug, women's risk of ever developing these problems is the same as men's (1992).

It is estimated that 20 percent of people who use marijuana at least monthly are daily smokers (Kleiman, 1989). Daily usage, although not always present in marijuana addiction, is an indicator of dependence or abuse.

Marijuana usage at levels as low as weekly may even become addictive, due to the build-up of $\Delta 9$-tetrahydrocannabinol (THC) in fatty tissues. Like DDT, the burden of THC in the body is cumulative because THC is 200 times more soluble in fat than in blood. Users ingest far more THC into the body than ever reaches the blood stream, and the elimination of its metabolites takes longer than a week. Many marijuana addicts in recovery report sustaining casual use for long periods before full-blown addiction developed; others' addiction progressed much more rapidly.

Marijuana and Health

Many harmful physical and psychological effects of marijuana have been found in addition to addiction. These include fetal effects, memory impairment, hormonal and gonadal disruption, lung disease and airway obstruction, increased risk of schizophrenia and relapse in stabilized patients, and various forms of cancers, including leukemia in children of marijuana smoking mothers (Nahas, 1993).

It is ironic that increased public awareness regarding cigarettes and other tobacco products has not been matched by heightened concern over marijuana. There have been several indications that marijuana is far more harmful to the body than cigarette smoke (Jones & Lovinger, 1985), and that marijuana causes pathological changes in the lungs (Fligiel et al., 1991).

Indications that marijuana compromises the immune system (Gold, 1989; Cabral & Vasquez, 1992/1993) are of particular concern today because of the pandemic of Human Immunodeficiency Virus (HIV) and Acquired Immune Deficiency Syndrome (AIDS). Marijuana use, like alcohol consumption, would also be expected to increase the risk that safer sex guidelines will not be followed due to euphoria or depression, poor judgment and memory, and in some cases, motor impairment.

Marijuana-related immune system impairment is also of concern because of the growing pool of drug resistant bacteriae, the wide range of chronic and acute viral diseases other than AIDS, growing concern over certain fungal infections, and increasing documentation of connections between immune system impairments and cancers.

Marijuana and Accidents

Marijuana was found in the blood of 34.7 percent of all trauma patients admitted to a Maryland trauma center in 1985-86 compared to only 32.6 percent testing positive for alcohol. Both substances were found in 16.5 percent of the subjects. Female subjects showed evidence of marijuana consumption 28.1 percent of the time and alcohol consumption in 21.1 percent of the cases (Soderstrom et al., 1988/1993). Although marijuana can be detected in the blood long after the "high" wears off, there is evidence that impairment of motor functions from one joint can last 24 hours (Leirer, Yesavage, & Morrow, 1993). These statistics, coupled with the wide-spread use of marijuana, suggest that there is a need to conduct public awareness campaigns about marijuana use and driving.

Use by a Family Member or Significant Other

As with any drug, marijuana use affects all significant relationships. Women are often introduced to marijuana by a husband or boyfriend, and using together becomes an important part of the relationship. Given the gap between the number of men and women who use weekly or more often, there are significant numbers of heterosexual relationships in which the man's use far exceeds the woman's. This is confirmed by anecdotal complaints found in newspapers' personal advice columns (Landers, 1991; Van Buren, 1989).

Despite the amount of attention given to co-dependency in recent years, marijuana has seldom been mentioned in this context. Partners of marijuana addicts need specific information about the effects of marijuana on relationships.

With the aging of cohorts which had the highest rates of use, family marijuana problems will be increasingly found at all ages. The old stereotype of a rebellious adolescent using marijuana in defiance of parental wishes is still representative of some families but many other patterns are emerging. Today, many parents use marijuana with their children and even grandchildren. An uncannily frequent fantasy of marijuana users is that they will eventually be puffing on a joint, sitting on a porch in their rocking chairs as senior citizens. If this fantasy is acted out in any numbers, family caregivers may be confronted by even more cases of senile memory loss than we are already seeing from Alzheimer's, strokes, and chronic alcohol use.

Marijuana use by parents should also be expected to lead to long-term adjustment problems among their children. Based on the experience of adult children of alcoholics, children of marijuana addicts will be suffering from the results of their parents' emotional remoteness, poor memory, and lack of coping skills for years.

Domestic Violence

Another gap in the literature is the lack of discussions of marijuana-related domestic violence. Kantor and Straus (1989) found that a husband's drug use was the most highly correlated risk factor for battered women. Although a marijuana addict is typically withdrawn and passive while high, there are reasons to think that marijuana may play a hidden role in domestic violence. Child abuse by marijuana-using parents should also be investigated.

Initially, marijuana is often used to relax, quiet anxiety, or deal with anger (Allen & West, 1968). Once an addict is habituated to the drug's effects, however, these emotions may return in a more difficult form. Paranoia, acute anxiety, and panic attacks are sometimes experienced under the influence of marijuana (Gold, 1989) and use may trigger more serious mental conditions. Addicts who are in mild or acute withdrawal can also be anxious, irritable, and moody. All of these effects have great potential for causing domestic violence.

Horrendous crimes have been committed by people with marijuana problems (Morain & Sahagun, 1989). Given the prevalence of domestic violence in our society, it is worthwhile looking into the possibility that marijuana may be contributing to it. Conversely, people who have used marijuana to cope with their aggressive feelings may need anger management training to abstain from marijuana without engaging in violent behavior.

Some evidence suggests that women's own use of marijuana may also correlate with a risk of being battered. A survey of women battered during pregnancy found that battered white, non-Latina women were twice as likely, and African American women were 4.7 times as likely to use marijuana as non-battered pregnant women. No information was provided on drug use by the batterer (Berenson et al., 1991). Finally, mothers of marijuana-affected adolescents face conflict and even violence in their homes. The National Family Partnership and various other parent support groups such as Toughlove have provided support for parents having problems of this kind. With the increase in adolescent marijuana use mentioned above and rising violence among youth, this problem may worsen.

Marijuana and Motherhood

Although perinatal drug issues have received a great deal of general attention in recent years, marijuana has not been singled out for the kind of attention paid to alcohol and cocaine. Nevertheless, marijuana is of concern both prenatally and during all phases of motherhood.

It is difficult to talk about mothers and potential mothers who use drugs, particularly illicit drugs, without shaming them. When raising concerns about marijuana use by mothers, professionals must tread a fine line between working to overcome denial in order to change behavior and creating a counterproductive burden of guilt. In this respect it may be helpful to remember that the higher the level of drug use and the greater the risk it entails, the less voluntary it is likely to be. Therefore, women who have difficulty abstaining from drugs during or after pregnancy are very likely addicted and must be treated with compassion despite whatever risk their use has caused their children.

Before conception, marijuana can diminish secretion of the luteinizing hormone which allows a fertilized egg to implant on the wall of the uterus. Other reproductive changes such as reduced or infrequent menses have also been found. Because marijuana is also believed to decrease the quantity and viability of sperm, couples where the man is a smoker may also have difficulty conceiving (Gold, 1989). Marijuana may be an under-recognized factor in the current epidemic of infertility.

A randomized sample of women giving birth in California in 1992 was tested for alcohol and other drugs at delivery. Marijuana was the most frequently found illicit drug, occurring in 1.88 percent of the total sample. African American and White women had the highest rates of marijuana use, 4.59 and 3.25 percent respectively. Latinas' rate of marijuana use was .61 percent, and Asian and Pacific Islander women had the lowest rate of prenatal marijuana use, .21 percent. Latinas and Asian women born in the U.S. had overall rates of illicit drug use closer to European American levels (Vega et al.).

Various fetal effects have been traced to marijuana use. It is believed that marijuana can produce birth defects similar to fetal alcohol syndrome (FAS). The combination of alcohol and marijuana has been found to produce a five-fold increase in the rate of FAS. Premature labor, low birth weight for gestational age and a distinctive, high pitched cry have been confirmed in mothers who smoked marijuana during pregnancy, as has an increased risk of a particular form of leukemia (Gold, 1989; Mondanaro, 1989).

Some marijuana-related problems have been noticed at birth, but seem to disappear shortly thereafter. Other problems might only be noticeable later in life. It is urgent that a longitudinal study be conducted to correlate health problems in the offspring of the many mothers in the U.S. today who have smoked marijuana before and during their pregnancies. This has been done in the case of the so-called DES babies, and is the only form of study which would be ethical given the nature of the problem. Such information is urgently needed to identify and quantify possible long-term effects of prenatal exposure to marijuana.

As a fat-soluble substance, THC has been detected in mothers' milk. Lactating women should be advised to abstain from marijuana at least as long as they nurse (Mondanaro, 1989).

Questions about marijuana and parenting which need investigation are the prevalence of child neglect and abuse by marijuana-affected parents, subtle impairments to parenting caused by marijuana, and stress to children who are told to conceal their parents' marijuana use from friends and authorities.

Marijuana Problems at Work

Marijuana is much better known as a problem in the world of work than in most other settings. Unfortunately, the focus on pre-employment and workplace drug-testing has obscured some of the more subtle issues of marijuana's effects on performance and safety.

A longitudinal study following adolescent subjects into young adulthood found that the problems caused by marijuana were comparable to the problems caused by alcohol. Whereas these young adults' six month prevalence rate for any alcohol use was more than twice the rate of any cannabis use, 90 percent for alcohol and 43 percent for marijuana, rates of use which were disruptive of their work or studies were almost the same for alcohol and pot, 18 percent for alcohol and 17 percent for marijuana. Young women's rate

of disruptive substance use was 27 percent compared to 39 percent
for young men in the study. The young women used marijuana at
work or school at a rate of 14.3 percent compared to 22.2 percent
for the males (Newcomb, 1988).

A controlled study of pre-employment drug screening among
2537 new postal employees found that those who had tested positive for marijuana had a 1.56 higher risk of turnover, a 1.55 higher
risk of accidents, a 1.85 higher risk of injuries, a 1.55 risk of discipline and an absentee rate 177.5 percent of non-users. Cocaine
users' risk for all of the categories shown above were the same or
lower than marijuana users except for a .02 higher risk of accidents
and a higher rate for absenteeism (Zwerling, Ryan, & Orav, 1990).

The high rates of THC found in the blood of patients at a trauma
center are relevant to many work situations. They are of particular
concern for drivers and equipment operators (Soderstrom et al.,
1993).

Blood levels of cannabis may not indicate use immediately prior
to the accident. However, this is less significant when the length of
time marijuana impairment can last after the "high" is considered.
Measurable errors were found in simulated aircraft landings by
seasoned pilots up to 24 hours after they had smoked a single
marijuana cigarette (Leirer, Yesavage, & Morrow, 1993).

Growing attention on urine testing and workplace detection has
rarely been matched by compassionate outreach to marijuana users.
Testing has too often been seen as a solution, taking attention away
from the humane, cost-effective, and proven strategies developed
by employee assistance programs. This is unfortunate because each
time a person with a marijuana problem is identified, there is a
chance to interrupt the disease of addiction at whatever stage it may
be. Women, as typically lower level and lower paid employees, may
be particularly vulnerable to workplace policies which do not include appropriate interventions or offers of recovery services.

MARIJUANA ADDICTION THEORY

Attitudes toward marijuana addiction in the professional community have reflected the ambivalence of the rest of our culture. In the
past, marijuana has seldom been included in discussions of addic-

tion per se. There is, however, a substantial and growing body of evidence that marijuana is an addictive drug.

The Myth of "Psychological Dependency"

The major form of professional denial regarding marijuana addiction has been the theory of "psychological dependency." This concept has been accepted as the correct scientific description of marijuana problems since the distinction between physical and psychological dependency was adopted by the World Health Organization in 1964[2] (Eddy et al., 1965).

There are two major problems with the belief that marijuana is only capable of producing psychological dependency. The first is that it is inaccurate even if the framework of dichotomizing physical and mental dependencies is accepted (Wikler, 1974; Harris, Dewey, & Razdan, 1977; Jones, Benowitz, & Herning, 1981; and Compton, Dewey, & Martin, 1990). Secondly, this framework is itself outdated (Jones, 1992).

Breaking Down Distinctions Between Physical and Psychological Addiction

In drug-taking, a *physical* substance consumed by the *body* alters *psychology*, the way the *mind* works. In order to have any effect on the mind, drugs have already crossed over the mind-body "barrier." For this reason, more and more researchers are realizing that the artificial distinction between the physical and the psychological does not work very well in the field of addiction (Brady et al., 1987).

Most currently accepted theories hold that addiction develops as a learned response to the intensely rewarding experiences some users derive from some drugs (O'Brien et al., 1992; Jaffe, 1992). The learning theory framework for addiction is simple, but not simplistic. Genetic, psychological, and environmental factors are all relevant to understanding why a given individual finds a particular drug rewarding and then goes on to become addicted to it. It is this interplay of factors which has led some researchers to use the term "biopsychosocial" for their models (Ewing, 1980; Galizio & Maisto, 1985).

*New Support for Marijuana's Classification
with Other Addictive Drugs*

The primary psychoactive component of marijuana, Δ9-tetrahy-drocannabinol (THC) has been demonstrated to act on the same neurotransmitter and brain reward systems as other addictive drugs (Gardner, 1992).[3] More recently, one marijuana-specific neurotransmitter has been isolated and christened "anandamide" (Swan, 1993), further supporting the classification of marijuana with other addictive drugs. Researchers believe that there may be other marijuana-like neurotransmitters as well.

Obsolete, Inadequate and Contradictory Research

There are many scientific reasons for the perpetuation of the myths of marijuana's harmlessness. Marijuana's increasing potency, difficulties with the design of animal studies, the cost of large-scale longitudinal and prospective studies, the length of time over which marijuana addiction typically develops, and the subtle nature of the impairment it causes have all contributed to research results which are misleading.

Unfortunately this continues. A recent example of an inadequate research design is a pharmacological study of supposedly daily marijuana smoking which used NIDA-approved marijuana cigarettes with only one percent THC, and studied six male volunteers smoking one cigarette daily for 13 consecutive days. Marijuana in common use today is from 10 to 15 times more potent than the variety used in this study, prompting some researchers to comment that it should be treated as an entirely new drug. Marijuana addicts often use daily for years before noticing physical problems, and it is common for them to smoke three or more joints a day. Even this unrealistic study design found increased heart rate as a negative effect (Perez-Reyes et al., 1991).

Lack of attention to marijuana compared to other drugs such as heroin and cocaine means that existing studies are often outdated and may not have been replicated. Many promising leads in older studies have not been followed up, and important research is left unpublicized.

Denial has also affected the way stated research results are used. Scientific discipline requires that results should only be given unequivocally when they are definitive and their significance has been established. However, use of this information for public information or by marijuana advocates has led to the impression that there is little evidence for marijuana's harmful effects or that they have even been disproved.

Another scientific source of denial regarding the potentially harmful effects of marijuana has been its therapeutic use in a few, relatively rare medical situations. Marijuana has been used to relieve loss of appetite associated with some chemotherapies and AIDS, and for glaucoma. Pro-marijuana groups have used this information to argue that marijuana has beneficial effects and should be legalized. They are sometimes joined by scientists and patients frustrated by the barriers to legitimate pharmacological uses of marijuana caused by drug laws.

Given the number of physical and mental problems which have been connected with chronic marijuana use, it is urgent that realistic research be conducted with chronic marijuana smokers who have used street grade marijuana daily for years. This would require ingenuity in the research design and the recruitment of large numbers of users. A research design of this type would overcome the legal prohibition on distributing high THC content marijuana and the difficulty of conducting long-range laboratory-based research. A large enough sample could compensate for the lack of individual reliability in addicts' reports of quantities and frequency of consumption. Such research should selectively study women and include sub-samples of various ages, ethnicities, reproductive status, and sexual orientations.

IMPLICATIONS FOR PUBLIC INFORMATION AND OUTREACH TO WOMEN

Improving public information and outreach is the first step toward helping women deal with their marijuana problems. In designing public information campaigns or materials for outreach, it is important that marijuana addiction be addressed specifically.

Two research studies found that people with marijuana problems would respond to outreach targeted specifically for them. Both studies were done to recruit subjects for research on chronic adult marijuana use. In one case women constituted 13.5 percent of respondents (Roffman & Barnhart, 1987) and in the other women represented 34.0 percent of the response (Hendin et al., 1987).

More research will need to be done to determine the most effective form of marijuana outreach for women. In seeking solutions, some help can be found in research on the prevention of alcohol problems among women. For example, Ferrence (1984) suggests that women's use of the health care system at rates greater than men and the design of specific outreach to meet women's social support needs can help reach women with alcohol problems.

Most public information materials currently in use perpetuate the myths and denial discussed above. Some admit that marijuana causes tolerance and withdrawal symptoms and still term marijuana addiction "psychological dependency." Many convey an equivocal message and cite conflicting research. This can feed the denial of a user who is experiencing problems and looking for help. It is extremely important to design new materials which make a clear statement regarding marijuana addiction.

One existing piece of public information literature which is clear and unequivocal is "Marijuana: Are the Highs Worth the Isolation?" published by Krames (1990). Although it portrays the marijuana addict as a male cartoon figure, it does discuss female reproductive issues and family problems with marijuana in more detail than any other piece of its kind.

Adolescent women, women of child-bearing age, women of the various ethnic groups, drivers, women who work with machinery and in hazardous settings, lesbians and bisexuals, and older women all need outreach and education materials designed to meet their particular marijuana-related needs.

DIAGNOSING MARIJUANA PROBLEMS

Once the myth that marijuana belongs in a different class of drugs is broken, diagnosis of marijuana addiction becomes much easier. As with any addiction, it is ideal if the person experiencing the problem identifies herself as an addict.

When this does not happen, a professional's opinion can help. A professional or family intervention can also lead an addict to accept that there is a problem. Johnson (1986) mentions marijuana problems specifically in his guide, *Intervention*, and Miller, Gold and Pottash (1989) recommend intervention for use with marijuana addicts.

Ironically, despite all the denial, being identified as an "addict" can be a big help to someone who has been struggling with marijuana-related problems or trying to control marijuana use alone. Addiction, while still carrying stigma, particularly for women, is at least a known quantity. Perhaps most importantly, it is generally accepted by the public that for an addict to recover, she or he will have to abstain from drugs.

Obstacles to Diagnosis of Marijuana Addiction

Marijuana addiction does pose some unique diagnostic problems. Professional resistance to treating marijuana like other drugs also affects the diagnostic tools available to clinicians.

DSM IV, like its predecessor, provides a "laundry list" of symptoms of which three or more must have persisted for a given period of time in order to diagnose substance dependence or abuse. Although these criteria are relevant for some marijuana addicts, DSM IV also requires a diagnosis to specify whether physiological dependence is present or not[4] (American Psychiatric Association, 1993). A "catch-22" situation arises in this regard because physiological dependence requires the presence of either tolerance or withdrawal symptoms, and there is no DSM IV category under which marijuana withdrawal can be diagnosed, even though nicotine withdrawal is given a classification!

The other difference in the fourth edition which is significant for marijuana addiction is the omission of criterion number four for psychoactive substance dependence from DSM-III-R. This criterion covered the performance of important obligations while intoxicated or in withdrawal, and applied to many marijuana addicts (American Psychiatric Association, 1987). These changes may make diagnosis of marijuana addiction more difficult.

Gold, the author of the only clinical handbook on marijuana addiction, found even the criteria for diagnosing substance abuse in

DSM III-R not very relevant to marijuana.[5] Gold states that he has found that "preoccupation with acquisition, compulsive use, and relapse" (1989, p. 101) are the three most reliable indicators that use of marijuana has crossed over into addiction.

Many of the difficulties in diagnosing marijuana addiction parallel problems with identifying alcoholism. This comparison can help focus attention away from physical symptoms onto the role of the drug in the person's life. No one would suggest today that a person is not an alcoholic just because she has not experienced shakes in the morning, liver disease, or hallucinations.

Length of Onset

Adult marijuana addicts have typically been using for many years before they are receptive to recovery. The mean age of subjects in one study of adult users was 31.5 years and the mean age at which they had begun daily use was 20.9. The range of ages at first daily use was 10 to 44. Female subjects averaged about a year older than the males with a range from 18 to 47 years (Roffman & Barnhart, 1987). In a subsequent treatment study sample, subjects had begun daily use at age 19.9 and had used for 15.39 years by the time they came to treatment (Stephens, Roffman, & Simpson, 1994).

Only one study in the literature provides data on the age at which women became daily users. In a study population of chronic marijuana users recruited through the media, 62.8 percent of female subjects were between 25 and 34 years of age and 62.9 percent of them had started daily use by the age of 21 (Hendin et al., 1987).

By the time most addicts "bottom out," marijuana has been a part of life so long that it is impossible for the clinician or the patient to compare their current moods, energy level or thought processes to pre-drug functioning. The length of time over which the problem has developed may be shorter if other drugs such as alcohol or cocaine have been used heavily, or if the addict is very young.

Denial

Much has already been said above about denial of marijuana addiction in cultural and professional settings. It is at the individual level, however, that the full impact of marijuana denial is felt. A woman may be particularly reluctant to accept that she is an addict.

Anecdotal evidence with marijuana and research on alcoholic women (Williams & Klerman, 1984) suggest that many women's use of marijuana involves a significant other who also has marijuana problems. In these situations, the woman's denial protects both her own use and her significant relationship.

Marijuana users also have developed positive rationalizations unique to this drug. Marijuana's "naturalness," the fact that it is used in religious groups including the Rastafarian, and its supposedly mind-expanding qualities are common elements in addicts' denial. Women from ethnic or cultural communities in which marijuana use is frequent may have a particularly hard time accepting a diagnosis from an outsider.

It can help overcome denial if a professional points out that just as some people who drink become alcoholics, some people who use marijuana get addicted to it. Thanks to public education, few people now question the existence of alcoholism, despite the large numbers of occasional drinkers.

The traditional 20 questions on alcoholism have been reframed for marijuana by Marijuana Anonymous, a relatively new 12-Step group (Marijuana Anonymous, undated). Such questions can help professionals, users, and their families identify life areas where marijuana use has become a problem.

Taking the Presence of Other Psychological Problems into Account

Women experience high rates of depression and seek help for mental problems at rates higher than men. This complicates designing appropriate substance abuse treatment for them (Braiker, 1984).

It may be difficult to distinguish between depression and marijuana addiction as the effects of chronic use often include low energy, flat affect, and depression. Marijuana can also mimic, trigger, or aggravate other psychiatric problems. As with assessments for other drug problems, when discussing marijuana use it is important to ask about pre-existing problems.

Once a diagnosis of marijuana addiction is made and recovery begins, care should be taken to follow up to see that depression is lifting. The length of marijuana detoxification discussed below can be very discouraging in this situation. Resumption of marijuana use has been linked to destablization of patients with other mental problems.

Intervening with Marijuana Addicts Who Are Functioning Well

Adult marijuana addicts are often apparently functional members of society. Despite daily, chronic marijuana use, many addicts are able to hold jobs and interact socially with others.

Mary Docter's case, quoted previously, shows that exceptional young adults may be able to study and carry out demanding physical tasks while using marijuana addictively. A case history in the only in-depth study of chronic daily adult marijuana smokers published to date was of a practicing lawyer. One of the female subjects was a successful writer. Both of these subjects avoided smoking before the end of work, however (Hendin et al., 1987).

Given this level of functioning, it is important that anyone preparing to diagnose marijuana addiction be prepared to answer the question "So what?"

The Hendin study team states that:

> We were impressed that marijuana permitted each of the individuals we studied to lead an unexamined life strikingly free of introspection. (p. 155)

> For some, like Jeffrey Gordon[6], . . . marijuana fostered a resigned acceptance of a lack of occupational success. Irene Rousseau and Emily Leone, who were reasonably successful in what they did but were operating well below their abilities, saw marijuana as enabling them to avoid the challenge of their own capabilities. For others, like Michael Forenzo, heavy marijuana smoking was part of a more total withdrawal from the competitive aggression of the working world and the responsibility for providing for his wife and family. (p. 157)

> When adult relationships were frustrating and painful, marijuana reduced anxiety, anger, and depression for these individuals. In facilitating their detachment from the unpleasant reality of a current situation, it enabled many of the subjects to exist for years in troubled relationships without feeling any urgency to do anything about them. (p. 158)

The use of marijuana to keep emotional distance was nowhere more evident than in the relationships between the heavy marijuana users and their children. Emily Leone was typical of mothers we saw who smoked while caring for their children, maintaining that rather than being an obstacle to a relationship, being high on marijuana relaxed them enough to enjoy being with their children. The strong objections their children had to their smoking suggested that the youngsters perceived that something quite different was going on. . . .On the other hand, Daniel Pollack, who did not smoke when with his children, treated them much as he did his employees, criticizing their performance in ways that inevitably alienated them from him. (p. 159)

We consistently observed their substitution of a sensory illusion of life for the boredom and fear of lifelessness that afflicted them. Such magical transformation became for many a substitute for the effort to real change. (p. 170)

Recovering marijuana addicts can be very effective in helping chronic users identify ways that marijuana is harming them by relating their experiences before recovery. Recovering addicts can also inspire hope by speaking from their own heart-felt relief about the positive changes abstinence has brought about.

Adolescent marijuana users may be more vulnerable to marijuana-induced impairment. Teens' incomplete physical and social development may place them at greater risk, and they may not have acquired the necessary skills to hide their impairment. Tennant (1985) has identified a post-drug impairment syndrome corresponding to anecdotal cases of drug "burn-out." This syndrome is more likely to affect people who became marijuana users at early ages.

WORKING WITH WOMEN IN RECOVERY FROM MARIJUANA ADDICTION

Once a woman has accepted that she has a marijuana problem or a diagnosis of addiction is made, it is imperative that appropriate support be available to her.

Finding Appropriate Services

Unfortunately, no models of marijuana-specific recovery programs for women are available.

Only one federally funded research program has focused on marijuana treatment. This program studied the effectiveness of relapse prevention training compared to social support group participation for paid subjects. A total of 10 sessions were held over a 12-week period, with abstinence expected by the fourth meeting. Women comprised 24.1 percent of the subjects and were not placed in separate women's groups. As a result of this intervention, 20 percent of subjects reported abstinence after a year. The women's 12-month rate was far lower than the men's, 11 percent compared to 24 percent (Stephens, Roffman, & Simpson, 1994).

The short period of time covered by the treatment program, the comparison of separate treatment components which are seen as complementary for other drugs, and the lack of an expectation of abstinence until well into the course of treatment make this study less helpful than might otherwise have been the case. It would be very interesting to see the effect of separate groups for women, of a research design combining relapse prevention training with social support groups, and of a longer or open-ended form of recovery services.

Clinicians working with this population have claimed that it was very helpful for marijuana addicts to be in groups where they could meet others who share their problem (McConnell, 1991). Miller, Gold, and Pottash (1989) mention the importance of this identification for marijuana addicts. Sharing experiences among marijuana addicts is the basis of the new marijuana-specific 12-step program, Marijuana Anonymous.

Zweben and O'Connell (1988) discuss strategies they have used to assist adult marijuana users to achieve abstinence in a substance abuse recovery setting. They offer several helpful suggestions for treatment. Among their recommendations are:

1. Education about marijuana, the withdrawal process and the meaning of craving;

2. Amino acid supplements including l-Tryptophan during detoxification and early recovery, particularly for clients with a family history of alcoholism;
3. Aerobic exercise no less than 30 minutes per session, at least four days a week;
4. Moderating the eating patterns of clients with mood swings;
5. Helping clients to clear their lungs of congestion through exercises and/or physical therapy;
6. Relapse prevention training, with use of the Behavioral Risk Scale developed by O'Connell (1985) particularly recommended;
7. Techniques to prevent or reduce sleep disturbances;
8. Urinalysis, even when not mandated by an employer or the legal system, as a support to the client's determination to stay clean and to family members' trust; and
9. Twelve-step program participation, ideally in the marijuana-specific groups which are beginning to form in some areas.

Denial of Marijuana Problems in Recovery Programs

Women with marijuana problems who find their way to community drug and alcohol recovery programs can encounter denial even there. Some drug counselors who focus on so-called "hard drugs" may minimize marijuana as "no big deal," particularly if they do not use a strict abstinence approach. Some community programs do not screen for marijuana when they do drug testing because of additional costs. Contact with other recovering participants in recovery programs also frequently supports the marijuana addict's denial. A newly clean and sober marijuana addict often hears statements such as: "If pot was my only problem, I'd still be out there."

Another important problem in substance abuse programs serving both men and women is the gender ratio in groups and activities. Co-sexual programs tend to recruit at least twice as many men as women unless they make extraordinary efforts to maintain balance. Women-only programs are scarce, and funding pressures in recent years have converted some general women's programs into perinatal services.

The Importance of Marijuana Specific 12-Step Programs

It is generally accepted that 12-step groups such as Alcoholics Anonymous (AA) represent an important resource for recovery. However, there are areas of the country where members of AA openly state that they smoke marijuana and still consider themselves sober.

Recently there has also been a tendency for AA groups in some areas to restrict members from mentioning drugs other than alcohol in meetings. This reflects the tremendous influx of polydrug users and alcoholics' desire to identify with the stories of those who share. However, this pressure can be detrimental for a marijuana addict/alcoholic who is used to denial. She may conclude from this that her marijuana problem is not real or important.

Narcotics Anonymous (NA) is another 12-Step resource to which many marijuana addicts have turned. However, denial of marijuana's addictive nature, or at least of its devastating effects, is even encountered in NA. Marijuana addicts may also feel uncomfortable in NA due to the value given by some NA groups to peers' histories of needle use, criminal acts, and time in jail. These reactions can feed the denial of "high bottom" marijuana addicts and help them reject the fellowship available there.

Marijuana Anonymous

Although many marijuana addicts have successfully recovered in AA and NA, many others have turned away. Marijuana addicts are like most newly sober addicts of all kinds: they are simultaneously trying to recover and looking for any excuse to return to using. Perhaps 12-Step groups' greatest accomplishment has been the concept of "one alcoholic (or addict) helping another." In this process, the newcomer's ability to identify with the most minute details of the using experiences of sober members is key. It is through this identification that the newcomer can believe that the clean and sober members of the fellowship have indeed once been in her or his condition and have overcome it.

A relatively new marijuana-specific 12-Step group, Marijuana Anonymous (MA), has been founded to address these issues. Although there are not enough meetings to fully support newly clean and sober marijuana addicts' recovery in many geographic areas, it is an important resource. MA is particularly appropriate for women in that it uses gender-neutral language in all of its materials. Contacts, materials, and meeting formats are available from MA World Services at P. O. Box 2912, Van Nuys, CA 91404.

Designing Marijuana-Appropriate Services for Women

The same considerations that apply to designing woman-specific and woman-sensitive programs for other drug problems are relevant to marijuana services. All areas of the program, facility, staffing, and management, should reflect a concern for women.

Recovery services should also take into account women's needs for support in coping with addiction-related problems. These include histories of rape, battering and childhood abuse. There are anecdotal indications that childhood sexual abuse is as common among female marijuana addicts as among other groups of addicted women. Marijuana addicts frequently come from alcoholic families, and thus face the issues associated with being adult children of alcoholics.

Practical barriers to women's participation in recovery programs also abound. Childcare responsibilities, objections from partners or family members, housework, more restrictive work situations, and a lack of disposable income for transportation and fees may all play roles in keeping women out of treatment or reducing access to it.

The author has found three currently available books particularly helpful in providing insights on women's chemical dependency problems and resources for designing women's services: *Feminism and Addiction* by Claudia Bepko (1991); the two volume publication *Alcohol and Drugs Are Women's Issues* (Roth, 1991); and the classic, *Alcohol Problems in Women* (Wilsnack & Beckman, 1984). Roth includes chapters and resources for working with various ethnic groups of women, and *Creating Visibility: Providing Lesbian-Sensitive and Lesbian-Specific Alcoholism Recovery Services* (Underhill, 1993) provides a training curriculum for substance abuse programs serving lesbians. A summary of important factors and strategies for designing women's services with references is available from the California Women's Commission on Alcohol and Drug Dependencies (undated).

There are only a few sources for ideas regarding marijuana-specific programming. The book by Gold (1989) and an article by Miller, Gold, and Pottash (1989) may be quite helpful although they focus on adolescent in-patient services. The two treatment modalities contrasted in research design by the Roffman group at the University of Washington might be helpful components in a program for marijuana recovery (Stephens, Roffman, & Simpson, 1994). Zweben and O'Connell (1988) also provide an excellent overview for recovery work with adult marijuana addicts.

Program elements which are particularly desirable for marijuana-addicted women are staffing by women who have experience with providing services to recovering marijuana addicts, marijuana-specific client education and information materials, and, if possible, a marijuana focused recovery group. Hazelden publishes a marijuana-specific recovery workbook which may be helpful in encouraging clients to write about their marijuana histories and in helping them to design marijuana-specific recovery plans (Nuckols, 1992).

These elements will also help women who do not initially identify as marijuana addicts. Many recovering people take a long time to fully assess their drug histories. Marijuana-specific information can help them realize the role the drug has played in their addiction and reduce the risk of relapse on marijuana.

Because THC is fat soluble, detoxing from heavy marijuana use takes longer than other drugs. Women who become abstinent from marijuana may not experience the "honeymoon" which helps some recovering alcoholics early in recovery. Six months or a year may pass before significant improvement in mood is felt, and this can be very discouraging.

Marijuana and Relapse

Marijuana has been identified as a significant factor in relapse. Chiauzzi (1991) mentions marijuana in several relapse contexts. One is the so-called marijuana maintenance program of some alcoholics and addicts who manage to avoid changing their behavior by substituting marijuana for their drug of choice. The smell of marijuana is also listed as a common trigger for drug craving.

Professionals working with marijuana addicts often see them relapse repeatedly. This may have to do with the length of detoxification; ease of access and social pressure to use marijuana in many school, work, entertainment, social, and family settings; persistent denial; or the high level of functioning many addicts have when they enter recovery. Marijuana addicts who have not shown extensive drinking histories often believe they can drink, and this can lead to marijuana relapse as well.

CONCLUSION

This article has presented several considerations relevant to women and marijuana. Hopefully, the comments presented here will interest others in the subject and lead to increased attention to this problem.

Summary of Recommendations Regarding Marijuana Programs and Services for Women

Outreach

The following elements are recommended for improving outreach to women regarding marijuana:

- Clear messages regarding risks of marijuana use including the term "addiction" in place of "psychological dependency";
- Dissemination of woman-specific marijuana information and prevention messages;
- Culturally oriented and sensitive materials designed for African American, Latina, Native American, Asian and Pacific Islander, differently abled, deaf, lesbian and bisexual women;
- Information for female partners of marijuana-using significant others;
- Attention to marijuana addiction as an adult problem;
- Realistic, positive prevention messages which:
  - present accurate information without exaggeration or denial of risks;

- acknowledge that some people seem to use marijuana safely but others DO develop addiction;
- empower adolescents and young adult women; and
- avoid parental, authority-based tactics.

Outreach Resources:

- Krames Communications brochure "Marijuana: Are the Highs Worth the Isolation?" (1990).
- For up-to-date, accurate marijuana information, particularly as it regards adolescents: The National Family Partnership, 11159-B S. Towne Square, St. Louis, MO 63123, (314) 845-1933, or PRIDE, 10 Park Place South, Suite 340, Atlanta, GA 30303.

Intervention

Marijuana-related information and appropriate intervention should be provided in settings where marijuana problems come to the attention of helping professionals such as:

- Schools;
- Health care sites;
- Mental health treatment;
- Perinatal clinics;
- Workplaces;
- Social services and support networks;
- Communities of religious faith;
- Rape and domestic violence survivor services; and
- Welfare, social security and other benefit systems.

Intervention Resource:

Vernon Johnson's 1986 book, *Intervention: How to Help Someone Who Doesn't Want Help.*

Treatment

Any program serving women should reflect women's needs in its:

• Recovery program design;
• Facility;
• Staff; and
• Management.

Features which are needed for women's marijuana-specific services include:

• Female staff, knowledgeable in women's marijuana problems;
• Women's recovery groups;
• Marijuana-specific addiction education;
• Marijuana-specific recovery materials;
• Marijuana-specific recovery discussion groups;
• Nutritional counseling and support including nutritional supplements;
• Exercise and physical therapy or instruction;
• Referrals to Marijuana 12-Step groups and other self-help groups as needed and available; and
• Relapse prevention training including information on the risk of relapse with marijuana.

Treatment Resources:

• *Feminism and Addiction,* by Claudia Bepko (1991);
• *Alcohol and Drugs Are Women's Issues,* edited by Roth, (1991);
• *Alcohol Problems in Women,* edited by Wilsnack and Beckman, (1984);
• *Creating Visibility: Providing Lesbian-Sensitive and Lesbian-Specific Alcoholism Recovery Services,* by Underhill (1993);
• "Women, Alcoholism, and Other Drugs: Factors to Consider in Recovery/Treatment," California Women's Commission on Alcohol and Drug Dependencies (undated);
• *Marijuana, Volume 1,* in *Drugs of Abuse, A Comprehensive Series for Clinicians*, by Gold (1989);

- "Strategies for Breaking Marijuana Dependence," by Zweben and O'Connell (1988); and
- "Treating Adult Marijuana Dependence, A Test of the Relapse Prevention Model," by Stephens, Roffman, and Simpson (1994).

Research

Areas which should receive immediate research attention include:

- Health effects of chronic marijuana use on women designed to study realistic levels of daily users' consumption over long periods of time;
- Outreach strategies which can attract women with marijuana problems into recovery;
- Comprehensive treatment models for female marijuana addicts;
- Longitudinal studies of children exposed to marijuana prenatally;
- The role of marijuana in domestic violence, child abuse and neglect, and problem parenting; and
- Prevention strategies to reduce marijuana problems among women, with particular attention to African American and pregnant women.

Given the lack of organized study, networking and cooperation among marijuana experts is sorely needed. Readers who find this information relevant to their experience are encouraged to correspond with the author.

With persistent interest in legalization or decriminalization of marijuana, it is urgent for chemical dependency professionals to speak out. It is not necessary to adopt a strict position of prohibition in order to do this. The public policy debate will be well served by any informed position which recognizes the devastation marijuana can cause to vulnerable individuals.

NOTES

1. The ethnic group titles used in the study are "Whites, Blacks, and Hispanics," but I have chosen to substitute the terms "European Americans, African Americans, and Latinas(os)" in response to recent dialogues regarding the importance of cultural heritage as compared to pigmentation and the desirability of self-definition.

2. At the same time, the term "addiction" was discarded even for use with heroin and other opiate problems but in the case of these drugs "dependency" was termed "physical."

3. Past confusion about marijuana's reward potential based on conflicting animal studies has been demonstrated by Gardner to have been the result of genetic differences between animal strains. Just as with humans, there are wide variations in animals' susceptibility to drug rewards.

4. This replaces the DSM-III-R severity index of "mild, moderate or severe." In light of the expansion of managed health care oversight of addiction services and attendant utilization review procedures, this change may make it more difficult to secure payment for marijuana addicts' treatment.

5. Gold provides an alternative list of signs and symptoms which can serve as cues of marijuana problems for a physician. Gold's list is more appropriate to the adolescent population than to adults. Items such as "frequent truancy," "suspicious robbery or breaking and entering while family is away," and "drug terminology in school notebooks or in yearbook inscriptions" would have to be revised for an adult population. Unfortunately, this bias perpetuates the myth that marijuana addiction is primarily an adolescent problem. The five extensive case reports he provides are also biased: all are for males between the ages of 16 and 19.

6. The names used in this quotation are fictitious. (Note added)

REFERENCES

Allen, J.R., & West, L.J. (1968). Flight from violence: Hippies and the green rebellion. *American Journal of Psychiatry, 125*(3), 120-126.

American Psychiatric Association. (1987). *Diagnostic and statistical manual of mental disorders (third edition-revised) DSM-III-R*. Washington, DC: American Psychiatric Association.

American Psychiatric Association. (1993). *DSM draft criteria*. Washington, DC: American Psychiatric Association.

Beckman, L.J., & Amaro, H. (1984). Patterns of women's use of alcohol treatment agencies. In S.C. Wilsnack & L.J. Beckman (Eds.), *Alcohol problems in women: Antecedents, consequences, and intervention* (pp. 319-348). New York: Guilford Press.

Bepko, C. (Ed.) (1991). *Feminism and addiction*. Binghamton, NY: The Haworth Press, Inc. [Reprinted from *Journal of Feminist Family Therapy, 3*(3/4)]

Berenson, A.B., Stiglich, N.J., Wilkinson, G.S., & Anderson, G.D. (1991). Drug abuse and other risk factors for physical abuse in pregnancy among white non-Hispanic, black, and Hispanic women. *American Journal of Obstetrics and Gynecology, 164*(6), 1491-1499.

Brady, J.V., Griffiths, R.R., Hienz, R.D., Ator, N.A., Lukas, S.E., & Lamb, R.J. (1987). Assessing drugs for abuse liability and dependence potential in laboratory primates. In M.A. Bozarth (Ed.), *Methods of assessing the reinforcing properties of abused drugs* (pp. 45-85). New York: Springer Verlag.

Braiker, H.B. (1984). Therapeutic issues in the treatment of alcoholic women. In S.C. Wilsnack, & L.J. Beckman (Eds.), *Alcohol problems in women: Antecedents, consequences, and intervention* (pp. 349-368). New York: Guilford Press.

Cabral, G.A., & Vasquez, R. (1993). Delta-9-tetrahydrocannabinol suppresses macrophage extrinsic anti-herpesvirus activity. In G.G. Nahas, & G. Latour (Eds.), *Cannabis: physiopathology, epidemiology, detection* (pp. 137-153). Boca Raton, FL: CRC Press (reprinted from *Proceedings Experimental Biology and Medicine*, 1992, *192*, 205-263).

California Women's Commission on Alcohol and Drug Dependencies (CWCADD). (undated). CWCADD Info alert: Women, alcoholism, and other drugs: Factors to consider in recovery/treatment. Available from CWCADD, 14622 Victory Blvd., Van Nuys, CA 91411.

Chiauzzi, E.J. (1991). *Preventing relapse in the addictions: A biopsychosocial approach*. New York: Pergamon.

Compton, D.R., Dewey, W.L., & Martin, B.R. (1990). Cannabis dependence and tolerance production. *Advances in Alcohol and Substance Abuse, 9*, 129-147.

Eddy, N.B., Halback, H., Isbell, H., & Seevers, M.H. (1965). Drug dependence: Its significance and characteristics. *Bulletin of the World Health Organization, 32*, 721-733.

Ewing, J.A. (1980). Biopsychosocial approaches to drinking and alcoholism. In W.E. Fann, I. Karacan, A.D. Pokorny, & R.L. Williams (Eds.), *Phenomenology and treatment of Alcoholism*. New York: Spectrum.

Ferrence, R.G. (1984). Prevention of alcohol problems in women. In S.C. Wilsnack, & L.J. Beckman (Eds.), *Alcohol problems in women: Antecedents, consequences, and intervention* (pp. 413-442). New York: Guilford Press.

Fligiel, S.E.G., Beals, T.F., Tashkin, D.P., Paule, M.G., Scallet, A.C., Ali, S.F., Bailey, J.R., & Slikker, W. (1991). Marijuana exposure and pulmonary alterations in primates. *Pharmacology Biochemistry & Behavior, 40*, 637-642.

Galizio, M.I., & Maisto, S.A. (1985). Determinants of substance abuse. New York: Plenum Press.

Gardner, E.L. (1992). Cannabinoid interaction with brain reward systems–The neurobiological basis of cannabinoid abuse. In L.L. Murphy, & A. Bartke (Eds.), *Marijuana/cannabinoids: Neurobiology and neurophysiology* (pp. 275-335). Boca Raton, FL: CRC Press.

Gasnier, L. (Director) (1936). *Reefer Madness* [Film]. Los Angeles, CA: United Artists Video.

Gilbert, B. (Producer), Higgins, C. (Director) (1980). *Nine to Five* [Film]. Farmington Hills, MI: CBS/Fox Video.

Gold, M.S. (1989). *Marijuana* (Drugs of abuse; Vol. 1). New York, NY: Plenum.

Harris, L.S., Dewey, W.L., & Razdan R.K. (1977). Cannabis: Its chemistry, pharmacology, and toxicology. In W.R. Martin (Ed.), *Drug addiction*. Berlin: Springer-Verlag.

Harvey, R. (1990, December 24). Docter moving back into life. *Los Angeles Times*, pp. C1, C2.

Hendin, H., Haas, A.P., Singer, P., Ellner, M., & Ulman, R. (1987). *Living high: daily marijuana use among adults*. New York: Human Sciences Press.

Increased use of marijuana and hallucinogens cited by PRIDE report. (1993). *The Alcoholism Report, 21*(9), 5-6.

Jacks, J. (Producer), Linlater, R. (Director) (1993). *Dazed and Confused* [Film]. Universal City, CA: Universal City Studios.

Jaffe, J.H. (1992). Current concepts of addiction. In C.P. O'Brien, & J.H. Jaffe (Eds.), *Addictive states* (pp. 1-21). New York: Raven Press.

Johnson, V. (1986). *Intervention: How to help someone who doesn't want help*. Minneapolis, MN: Johnson Institute.

Jones, H.C., & Lovinger, P.W. (1985). *The marijuana question and science's search for an answer*. New York: Dodd, Mead & Company.

Jones, R.T. (1992). What have we learned from nicotine, cocaine, and marijuana about addiction? In C.P. O'Brien, & J.H. Jaffe (Eds.), *Addictive states* (pp. 109-122). New York: Raven Press.

Jones, R.T., Benowitz, N.L., & Herning, R.I. (1981). Clinical relevance of cannabis tolerance and dependence. *Journal of Clinical Pharmacology, 21*, 143S-152S.

Kandel, D.B. (1992). Epidemiological trends and implications for understanding the nature of addiction. In C.P. O'Brien, & J.H. Jaffe (Eds.), *Addictive states* (pp. 23-39). New York: Raven Press.

Kantor, G.K., & Straus, M.A. (1989). Substance abuse as a precipitant of wife abuse victimizations. *American Journal of Drug and Alcohol Abuse, 15*(2), 173-189.

Kleiman, M.A. (1989). *Marijuana: costs of abuse, costs of control*. Westport, CT: Greenwood Press.

Krames Communications (1990). *Marijuana: Are the highs worth the isolation?* San Bruno, CA: Krames Communications.

Landers, A. (1991, April 14). Stopping 2 'terrific guys' from going to pot. *Los Angeles Times* (E12).

Leirer, V.O., Yesavage, J.A., & Morrow, D.G. (1993). Marijuana carry-over effects on psychomotor performance: a chronicle of research. In G.G. Nahas, & C. Latour, (Eds.), *Cannabis: physiopathology, epidemiology, detection* (pp. 47-60). Boca Raton, FL: CRC Press.

Marijuana Anonymous. (undated). Addicted to marijuana? Twenty Questions. Available from MA World Service, P.O. Box 2912, Van Nuys, CA 91404.

McConnell, H. (1991). "It's kind of lonely": Many marijuana users need help. *The Journal, 20*(3), 1. Toronto: Addiction Research Foundation.

McKirnan, D.J., & Peterson, P.L. (1992). Gay and lesbian alcohol use: Epidemiological and psychosocial perspectives. In EMT Group Inc. (Ed.), *Proceedings*.

The research symposium on alcohol and other drug problem prevention among lesbians and gay men (pp. 61-84). Sacramento, CA: California Department of Alcohol and Drug Programs.

Miller, S.N., Gold, M.S., & Pottash, A.C. (1989). A 12-step treatment approach for marijuana *(cannabis)* dependence. *Journal of Substance Abuse Treatment, 6,* 241-250.

Mondanaro, J. (1989). *Chemically dependent women: Assessment and treatment.* Lexington, MA: Lexington Books.

Morain, D., & Sahagun, L. (1989, January 20). Escalating hate reportedly consumed gunman. *Los Angeles Times,* Part I, pp. 3, 38.

Moritz, N., & Heyman, D. (Producers), Melkonian, J. (Director) (1993). *The Stoned Age* [Film]. Trimark Pictures.

Nahas, G.G. (1993). General toxicity of cannabis. In G.G. Nahas, & C. Latour (Eds.), *Cannabis: physiopathology, epidemiology, detection* (pp. 5-17). Boca Raton, FL: CRC Press.

National Clearinghouse for Alcohol and Drug Information. (1989). Alcohol and other drug use in three Hispanic populations: Mexican-Americans, Puerto Ricans, and Cuban-Americans. (Data source, National Institute on Drug Abuse, 1987.) In *NCADI update, January 1989* (MS 376). Rockville, MD: NCADI.

Newcomb, M.D. (1988). *Drug use in the workplace: risk factors for disruptive substance use among young adults.* Dover, MA: Auburn House.

Norton, R., & Colliver, J. (1988). Prevalence and patterns of combined alcohol and marijuana use. *Journal of Studies on Alcohol, 49*(4), 378-380.

Nuckols, C.C. (1992). Quitting marijuana: Your personal recovery plan (Order No. 5518). Center City, MN: Hazelden.

O'Brien, C.P., Childress, A.R., McLellan, A.T., & Ehrman, R. (1992). A learning model of addiction. In C.P. O'Brien, & J.H. Jaffe (Eds.), *Addictive states* (pp. 157-177). New York: Raven Press.

O'Connell, K.R. (1985). *End of the Line: Quitting Cocaine.* Philadelphia: Westminster.

Perez-Reyes, M., White, W.R., McDonald, S.A., Hicks, R.E., Jeffcoat, A.R., & Cook, C.E. (1991). The pharmacologic effects of daily marijuana smoking in humans. *Pharmacology Biochemistry & Behavior, 40,* 691-694.

Roffman, R.A., & Barnhart, R. (1987). Assessing need for marijuana dependence treatment through an anonymous telephone interview. *The International Journal of the Addictions, 22*(7), 639-651.

Roth, P. (1991). *Alcohol and drugs are women's issues: Vol. 1, A review of the issues: Vol. 2, The model program guide.* Metuchen, NJ: Women's Addiction Alliance & The Scarecrow Press.

Skinner, W., & Otis, M.D. (1992). Drug use among lesbian and gay people: findings, research design, insights, and policy issues from the Trilogy Project. In EMT Group Inc. (Ed.), *Proceedings. The research symposium on alcohol and other drug problem prevention among lesbians and gay men* (pp. 34-60). Sacramento, CA: California Department of Alcohol and Drug Programs.

Soderstrom, C.A., Trifillis, A.L., Shankar, B.S., Clark, W.E., & Cowley, A. (1993). Marijuana and alcohol use among 1023 trauma patients. In G.G. Nahas, & C. Latour (Eds.), *Cannabis: physiopathology, epidemiology, detection* (pp. 79-92). Boca Raton, FL: CRC Press, (reprinted from *Archives of surgery*, 1988, *123*, 733-737).

Stephens, R.S., Roffman, R.A., & Simpson, E.E. (1994). Treating adult marijuana dependence: A test of the relapse prevention model. *Journal of Consulting and Clinical Psychology, 62*(1), 92-99.

Substance Abuse and Mental Health Services Administration. (1993). *National household survey on drug abuse: Population estimates 1992* (DHHS Publication No. SMA 93-2053). Rockville, MD: U.S. Dept. of Health and Human Services, Public Health Service, SAMHSA, Office of Applied Studies.

Swan, N. (1993). Researchers make pivotal marijuana and heroin discoveries. In National Institute on Drug Abuse, *NIDA notes, 8*(4), pp. 1 & 4. Washington, DC: National Institutes of Health.

Tennant, F. (1985). Post Drug Impairment Syndrome (PDIS). (Available from: Veract, 338 S. Glendora Ave., W. Covina, CA, 91790).

Underhill, B.L. (1993). *Creating visibility: Providing lesbian-sensitive and lesbian-specific alcoholism recovery services*. Los Angeles: Alcoholism Center for Women, 1147 S. Alvarado St., 90006.

Van Buren, A. (1989, February 3). A wedding with a special ring to it. *Los Angeles Times,* Part V, p. 3.

Vandor, M., Juliana, P., & Leone, R. (1991). Women and illegal drugs. In P. Roth (Ed.), *Alcohol and drugs are women's issues: Vol. 1, A review of the issues*. Metuchen, NJ: Women's Addiction Alliance & Scarecrow Press.

Vega, W.A., Noble, A., Kolody, B., Porter, P., Hwang, J., & Bole, A. (1993). *Profile of alcohol and drug use during pregnancy in California, 1992*. (Publication No. ADP 93-571.) Sacramento, CA: California Department of Alcohol and Drug Programs.

Wickler, A. (1974). The marijuana controversy. In L. Miller (Ed.), *Marijuana: effects on human behavior*. New York: Academic Press, a subsidiary of Harcourt Brace Jovanovich.

Williams, C.N., & Klerman, L.V. (1984). Female alcohol abuse: Its effects on the family. In S.C. Wilsnack, & L.J. Beckman (Eds.), *Alcohol problems in women: Antecedents, consequences, and intervention*. New York: Guilford Press.

Wilsnack, S.C., & Beckman, L.J. (Eds.). (1984). *Alcohol problems in women: Antecedents, consequences, and intervention*. New York: Guilford Press.

Zweben, J.E., & O'Connell, K. (1988). Strategies for breaking marijuana dependence. *Journal of Psychoactive Drugs, 20*(1), 121-127.

Zwerling, C., Ryan, J., & Orav, E.J. (1990). The efficacy of preemployment drug screening for marijuana and cocaine in predicting employment outcome. *Journal of the American Medical Association, 264*(20), 2639-2643.

Index

AA (Alcoholics Anonymous), 156
ACOAs. *See* Adult children of
    alcoholics (ACOAs)
Adult children of alcoholics
    (ACOAs)
    lesbian women trauma of, 91
    self-perception alterations of, 94
Affect regulation, of lesbian
    alcoholism trauma, 92-93
African Americans
    countertransference toward, 75-
        76
    "family" composition of, 26
    female circumcision of, 76
    marijuana use rates of, 134,135,
        141,142
    mobility denial to, 71
    self-identity crisis of, 71
Aid to Families with Dependent
    Children (AFDC), xv
AIDS. *See* HIV/AIDS
*Alcohol and Drugs are Women's
    Issues* (Roth), 157,161
Alcohol Problems in Women
    (Wilsnack & Beckman),
    157,161
Alcoholics Anonymous (AA), 156
Alexithymia
    somatic symptoms and, 97
    of trauma survivors, 93
Amnesia, of lesbian alcoholism
    trauma, 93
Anandamide, marijuana
    neurotransmitter, 146
Anhedonia, of trauma survivors, 93
Asian women, marijuana use rates
    of, 136,142

Barriers to treatment
    childcare services availability, 14
    environmental barriers, 15
    individual barriers, 15
    opposition of family and friends,
        14,133
    physical/sexual abuse, xiv
Behavioral Risk Scale, 155
Bio-psycho-social-spiritual disease,
    of addiction, xvii
Bisexual women
    marijuana use rates of, 137
    population specific services to, 13
    See also Lesbian women

California Women's Commission on
    Alcohol and Drug
    Dependencies, 157,161
Child care services
    lack of during treatment, 14
    retention factor of, 49
Codependence
    disease model of, 36-37
    HIV risk and, 113
    marijuana use and, 140
    relationship devaluation in, 36
    unequal, nonmutual relationships
        and, 37
Complex Post-Traumatic Stress
    Disorder concept, 91-92
Connected knowing female learning
    style, 25-26
    intimate relationship drug use
        and, 31
Consciousness regulation, of lesbian
    alcoholism trauma, 93-94
Countertransference
    aggression and, 76
    ethno-cultural identity and, 75-76
    guilt and, 76

169

MA (Marijuana Anonymous), 151,
　154,156-57
Marijuana Anonymous (MA), 151,
　154,156-57
Marijuana problems of women
　background on, 130
　conclusions regarding
　　intervention, 160
　　outreach, 129-30,159-60
　　research, 129,162
　　treatment, 161-62
　denial and, 14,129,130-33
　　counterproductive prevention
　　　efforts and, 132
　　diagnosis obstacles of, 149,
　　　150-51
　　"gateway drug" concept and,
　　　132
　　legalization/decriminalization
　　　issue and, 131
　　medicinal use issue and, 131,
　　　147
　　outreach efforts and, 148
　　rebellious attitude
　　　reinforcement and, 132
　　in recovery programs, 155-57
　　research results and, 147
　　treatment opposition by family
　　　and, 133
　　youth counter-culture
　　　development and, 131
　diagnosis obstacles and
　　denial, 149,150-51
　　drug classification, 148
　　DSM-III-R and DSM-IV
　　　criteria, 149-150,163
　　high functioning intervention,
　　　152-53
　　length of onset, 150
　　other psychological problems,
　　　151-52
　epidemiology of
　　African American use rates,
　　　134,135,141,142

　　Asian and Pacific Islander use
　　　rates, 136,142
　　ethnic use by age groups, 137
　　European American use rates,
　　　134,135,136,142
　　Latinas use rates, 135,136,141,
　　　142
　　lesbian and bisexual use rates,
　　　135,137
　　Native American use rates,
　　　135,136
　　youth use increase and,
　　　137-38,141,153
　marijuana addiction theory and,
　　144-47
　outreach regarding, 129-30,
　　147-48, 148,159-60
　parenting and, 129,138,140,
　　143-43,153
　post-drug impairment syndrome
　　and, 153
　pregnancy and, 129,136,141,
　　142-43
　psychological dependency myth
　　and, 159
　　addictive drug classification
　　　and, 146,159
　　physical vs. psychological
　　　addiction and, 145,148
　　research obsolescence and,
　　　129,130-31,146-47,162
　recovery from
　　12-step programs and, 154,
　　　155,156-57
　　denial in recovery programs
　　　and, 155-57
　　gender ratio problems and, 155
　　Marijuana Anonymous and,
　　　151,154,156-57
　　relapse and, 158-59
　　services for, 153-55,157-58,
　　　161
　specific issues of, 138-39
　　accident prevalence, 139-40
　　domestic violence, 141

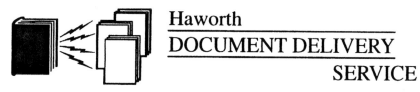

Haworth
DOCUMENT DELIVERY
SERVICE

This valuable service provides a single-article order form for any article from a Haworth journal.

- *Time Saving:* No running around from library to library to find a specific article.
- *Cost Effective:* All costs are kept down to a minimum.
- *Fast Delivery:* Choose from several options, including same-day FAX.
- *No Copyright Hassles:* You will be supplied by the original publisher.
- *Easy Payment:* Choose from several easy payment methods.

Open Accounts Welcome for . . .
- Library Interlibrary Loan Departments
- Library Network/Consortia Wishing to Provide Single-Article Services
- Indexing/Abstracting Services with Single Article Provision Services
- Document Provision Brokers and Freelance Information Service Providers

MAIL or *FAX* THIS ENTIRE ORDER FORM TO:

Haworth Document Delivery Service
The Haworth Press, Inc.
10 Alice Street
Binghamton, NY 13904-1580

or FAX: 1-800-895-0582
or CALL: 1-800-342-9678
9am-5pm EST

PLEASE SEND ME PHOTOCOPIES OF THE FOLLOWING SINGLE ARTICLES:
1) Journal Title: _____
    Vol/Issue/Year: _____ Starting & Ending Pages: _____
    Article Title: _____

2) Journal Title: _____
    Vol/Issue/Year: _____ Starting & Ending Pages: _____
    Article Title: _____

3) Journal Title: _____
    Vol/Issue/Year: _____ Starting & Ending Pages: _____
    Article Title: _____

4) Journal Title: _____
    Vol/Issue/Year: _____ Starting & Ending Pages: _____
    Article Title: _____

(See other side for Costs and Payment Information)

COSTS: Please figure your cost to order quality copies of an article.

1. Set-up charge per article: $8.00
   ($8.00 × number of separate articles)   _____

2. Photocopying charge for each article:

       1-10 pages: $1.00   _____

       11-19 pages: $3.00   _____

       20-29 pages: $5.00   _____

       30+ pages: $2.00/10 pages   _____

3. Flexicover (optional): $2.00/article   _____

4. Postage & Handling: US: $1.00 for the first article/

       $.50 each additional article   _____

       Federal Express: $25.00   _____

       Outside US: $2.00 for first article/

       $.50 each additional article_____

5. Same-day FAX service: $.35 per page   _____

           GRAND TOTAL: _____

METHOD OF PAYMENT: (please check one)

❑ Check enclosed   ❑ Please ship and bill. PO # _____
           (sorry we can ship and bill to bookstores only! All others must pre-pay)

❑ Charge to my credit card: ❑ Visa;   ❑ MasterCard; ❑ Discover;
           ❑ American Express;

Account Number:_____ Expiration date:_____

Signature: ✗ _____

Name: _____ Institution: _____

Address: _____

_____

City: _____ State:_____ Zip:_____

Phone Number: _____ FAX Number: _____

MAIL or *FAX* THIS ENTIRE ORDER FORM TO:

Haworth Document Delivery Service	**or FAX:** 1-800-895-0582
The Haworth Press, Inc.	**or CALL:** 1-800-342-9678
10 Alice Street	9am-5pm EST)
Binghamton, NY 13904-1580	